Chicago
and
Other Plays

Other Plays by Sam Shepard

Action
Angel City
Back Bog Beast Bait
Buried Child
Cowboy Mouth
Cowboys #2
Curse of the Starving Class
Forensic and the Navigators
Geography of a Horse Dreamer
The Holy Ghostly
Killer's Head
La Turista
The Mad Dog Blues
Operation Sidewinder
The Rock Garden
Seduced
Shaved Splits
Suicide in B♭
The Tooth of Crime
The Unseen Hand
4-H Club

Chicago

Icarus's Mother

Red Cross

Fourteen Hundred Thousand

Melodrama Play

Sam Shepard

APPLAUSE
THEATRE BOOK PUBLISHERS
100 West 67 St. • New York. N.Y. 10023 • (212) 496-7511
BN: 0-87910-205-5
$ 9.95

Library of Congress Cataloging in Publication Data

Shepard, Sam, 1943–
   Chicago and other plays.

   Reprint of the 1967 ed. published by Bobbs-
Merrill, Indianapolis, under title: Five plays.
   CONTENTS: Chicago.--Icarus's mother.--Red
cross.--Fourteen hundred thousand.--Melodrama
play.
   I. Title.
(PS3669.H394F5 1981)   812'.54   80-27632
ISBN 0-89396-042-X
ISBN 0-89396-043-8 (pbk.)

Contents

14511

Chicago

CHICAGO was first produced at Theatre Genesis. It was directed by Ralph Cook and played by Warren Finnerty, Kevin O'Connor, Lyn Hutt, Lee Kissman, Susanne English, Lenette Reuben, and Paul Plummer; it was subsequently produced by Ellen Stewart in a La Mama repertory European tour, and by the Avanté Productions Theatre in Los Angeles.

NOTES ON *CHICAGO*

Sam Shepard's plays are the most totally realized in original script of any writer I have directed. In every argument I have ever had with him, about staging, use of sound, interpretation, etc., Sam has always been right. He has an instinctive sense of what is theatrically right for his plays that goes beyond rules and preconceptions. He is a great poet in both literary and theatrical imagery.

In the Genesis production of *Chicago* the only continuously real elements were Stu, a bathtub, a towel, and soap. The other actors, offstage rooms, and props, etc., were forces working upon his reality. In other words, the bathtub is not in a bathroom; it exists on a stage in front of an audience. The set is black and as perfectly symmetrical and simple as possible with stage left and stage right entrances. The offstage party sounds are heard only when Stu hears them. The sense should be that the sounds continue, but we perceive them only when Stu does. Of course, even this creates a certain kind of reality which is utterly destroyed when the guests become fishermen. The movement of the play is from Stu's minute particular subjective problem (i.e., Joy's leaving Stu, and the threat of his being chopped if he follows her) to the universal problem of Man's being civilized to the suffocating point of losing his balls. To stay on the beach is death; to go up the hill is death. The play ends with Stu's acceptance of death as the only means of birth.

Ralph Cook

2

SCENE

(The lights dim down in the house. A POLICEMAN *comes out in front of the curtain with a club. He beats the curtain several times with the club, then walks into the audience and up the center aisle. He goes to the back of the house and bangs his club three times on the back of a chair. Someone reciting the "Gettysburg Address" comes on very loudly through the sound system. The curtains open. The lights come up slowly on a bare stage. Upstage center* STU *is sitting in a bathtub splashing water and talking in a singsong manner. The "Gettysburg Address" fades out as* STU *continues.)*

STU

And ya' walk through the town. With yer head on the ground. And ya' look all around through the town fer yer dog. Your dog Brown. He's yellow but ya' call him Brown anyhow. And sit in the hay. And ya' say. What a day. This is it. It's the day that ya' say is okay. Anyway. Anyhow. You know by now. That yer dog is dead and ya' don't care anyhow. 'Cause ya' didn't really like him in the first place. So ya' say. What a day. In the hay. Anyway. And ya' walk through the town and around. Then ya' see another tree. And ya' pee on the ground. 'Cause it's nice and ya' don't think twice. Ya' just do and it's done. And it's fun. Ho, ho.

JOY

(Off right) Biscuits!

STU

Biscuits in the sun. And ya' run. And it's fun. Ya' have a gun. It's yer own. Ya' don't care. You can even shoot a bear. If ya' have any hair. If ya' don't. Ya' don't. If ya' do. It's true. And yer through anywho.

3

JOY

(*Off right*) Biscuits are ready!

STU

Teddy and Freddy and all the stupid people having fun with a gun. And ya' run all around. Through the town. What a way. To spend a day. In the hay. By the way. It's okay. Stay away. (JOY *comes on from right in a bathrobe; she yells at* STU.)

JOY

Biscuits! Biscuits! Come on! (*She goes off right.* STU *stands suddenly in the bathtub; he is wearing long pants and tennis shoes without a shirt.*)

STU

Just a second! Just a second! (JOY *comes back on from right.*)

JOY

What?

STU

A towel.

JOY

Just a second. (*She goes off right.*)

STU

If it was warm I could go without a towel. Seeing as how it's cold, I'll need one. (JOY *comes back on with a towel; she throws it at* STU, *then goes back off right.* STU *stays standing up in the tub drying himself.*) Thanks.

JOY

(*Off right*) Okay.

STU

I meant if the sun were out. That kind of warmth. Not

4

just warm but a sun kind of warmth. You know? Like the beach.

JOY

(*Off right*) The beach has sun.

STU

I know. You just lie there and the sun dries you and the sand gets all stuck to you. It sticks all over. In your toes. In your ears. Up your crotch. Aaah! Sand between your legs! Aaah! Sticking in your pores. Goddamn! (*He sits back down in the tub and puts the towel over his head; he talks like an old lady, using the towel as a bandanna.*) All you young little girlies out there paradin' around in yer flimsies. Makes me all ashamed and pink in the face to think a' that.

JOY

(*Off right*) What?

STU

Two-pieces and one-pieces and bare-chested things going on. No upbringin'. That's it. That's where it comes from. A lack a' concern on the part a' the parents and all. Flimsy morality. Dirty shame. (JOY *comes on fast from right.*)

JOY

Cold biscuits! Do you dig cold biscuits? The butter's cold, too. The jam's cold. I hope you're glad. (*She goes off right.* STU *stands again with the towel still draped over his head; he talks like an old lady.*)

STU

Looky here, missy. Don't be so high and mighty and flashy, all of a sudden. Just 'cause ya' got big boobies. Thank the Lord fer that. But that happens to be a gift.

5

Ya' were bestowed with that chest a' yours. And don't forget it. Praise the Lord!

JOY

(*Off right*) Fuck off! (STU *takes the towel off his head and starts drying himself again; he talks in a normal voice.*)

STU

Biscuits. Who needs biscuits at this hour? Who ever needs biscuits? Joy?

JOY

(*Off right*) What?

STU

Who needs biscuits?

JOY

Peasants in Mexico.

STU

Peasants make their own. Biscuits were invented to trick people into believing they're really eating food! They aren't any good at all. They're just dough. A hunk of dough that goes down and makes a gooey ball in your stomach. It makes you feel full. Biscuits are shit! (JOY *throws a bunch of biscuits from off right; they hit* STU *in the head,* STU *picks one up and takes a bite out of it, he sits back down in the tub and continues eating the biscuit; a phone rings off left,* JOY *crosses the stage and exits left still wearing the nightgown, she answers the phone, she talks off left.*)

JOY

Hello. Hi. Oh, you're kidding. Is that right? Oh Myra. Well when's he leaving? He left? He's gone? You do? Oh fine. Yes. I got the job. Yes, it's final. Well they called last night. Last night. Uh-huh. Two weeks. A week maybe. The sooner the better. I'll see. Well I have a few things to do. Yes. Okay. 'Bye. (*She hangs up; she comes on from left dressed in a bra and slip, she crosses the stage.*) How's your biscuit?

STU
Good. How's yours? (*She exits right.*)

JOY
(*Off right*) Myra's coming.

STU
Did you say you got the job? Did I hear you say that?

JOY
I said Myra's coming.

STU
On the phone. Did you say you got the job?

JOY
Yes. (STU *stands suddenly in the tub and starts yelling.*)

STU
You did not!

JOY
(*Off right*) Yes!

STU
They hired you!

JOY
Yes!

STU
Good! I'm really glad!

JOY
Good!

STU
I'm really, really glad. When are you going? (JOY comes *on from right brushing her hair and still wearing the bra and slip.*)

JOY
Oh I don't know.

STU
You don't?

JOY
Soon.

STU
Good. (JOY *climbs into the tub with* STU.) Don't! You can't get in here.

JOY
How come?

STU
Because there's not enough water.

JOY
Don't be stupid. We can fill it up.

STU
It'll overflow.

JOY
Myra's coming.

STU
You told me. (JOY *kisses* STU; *they embrace for a while, then sit in the tub facing each other;* JOY *brushes her hair.*)

JOY
It's really nice out here.

STU
Out where?

JOY
On the water.

STU
(*Putting the towel on his head and talking like an old lady*) All you young things are the same. Corny. Corny young girls. That's what.

JOY
I love the water.

STU
Ya' all love the water. Water in the nighttime. With the moon hangin' over yer filthy little head.

JOY
It's so quiet.

STU
Yeah. Ya' like the quiet 'cause ya' don't take the time to listen when it's not quiet.

JOY
Listen to the waves.

STU
Listen yerself, missy. I heard water slappin' on the pier before. I got ears.

JOY
I could stay here forever. Feel the breeze.

STU
A corny young virgin. That's what.

JOY
It's so nice. (*She leans over the side of the tub as though it were a boat.*)

9

STU
Nice, nice. No nicer than most things.

JOY
Look at the fish. (STU *leans over and looks.*)

STU
Them's barracuda, lady. They eat people when they feel like it.

JOY
They wouldn't eat me.

STU
They'd eat you like nobody's business.

JOY
They're really big.

STU
Big as they come. (MYRA *comes on from left dressed in a fur coat and dark glasses and carrying a suitcase. She stands looking on.*)

JOY
That's awful.

STU
See the way they flash around. That's 'cause they're hungry.

JOY
Really?

STU
Starvin' to death.

JOY
Damn.

10

STU
Just lookin' fer a nice young virgin.

JOY
They don't eat people.

STU
Just lookin' fer somethin' to bite. (*He grabs her and tries to push her out of the tub.*)

JOY
Stop it!

STU
All them fishies gettin' ready fer a feast.

JOY
Cut it out! (*They stand struggling with each other.*)

STU
Big striped fishes with long teeth and pink tongues.

JOY
Stop!

STU
(*Normal voice*) They like you. They want you for their very own. They want to eat you up!

JOY
No! (*They kiss for a while.*)

STU
Myra's here.

MYRA
Hello, Joy. Are you ready?

JOY
No.

STU

She's ready.

JOY

I am not.

STU

She got hired. (JOY *climbs out of the tub and starts brushing her hair.*)

MYRA

It's a good job.

JOY

It's all right. (JOY *exits right brushing her hair,* MYRA *follows behind her, they go off.* STU *stands looking down at the floor.*)

STU

Tough luck, fish. You're really ugly anyway. Eat some little fish. Minnows or something. Seaweed. Try some seaweed for a change. You're going to be in bad shape if you keep going around like that. In schools. In all that crappy black water. Bumping your dumb heads into rocks and boulders and making your tongues bleed. Stupid. Swim. Go ahead. Let me see you. Don't just hang there treading water. (*He kneels down in the tub looking over the edge.*) What's wrong? I see you, stupid. Go down. Dive or something. Beat it! All right! Stay there. See if I care. (*He lies back in the tub and puts his feet up on the edge.*) You can't wait forever. You'll have to go when it gets dark. People will start looking for you when it gets dark. They'll be out in boats. They'll have long hip boots on and pipes and mosquito juice on their faces. They'll have bottles of worms and poles for you. They'll get in all their little boats and push them out in the water. Then they'll whisper to each other about what a nice night it is and how still it is and look at all the fireflies. Then they'll row very softly out to the middle. Out in the deep part. And they'll break out their thermos bottles full of coffee and split pea soup. And they'll drink and whisper about you. About how big you are and how striped you are and how nice it would be to have your head cut off and mounted over the fireplace. They'll get out their poles and the worms and the hooks and drop them over the side. The worm will just float for a while, then he'll have a little spasm and wriggle on the hook. Then he'll drown and sink all the way to the bottom and die in front of your long noses. You'll watch him for a while, see. Then you'll move a little bit. You're pretty hungry but you're not sure. So you take your time. You're down there moving slowly around this worm, taking your time. And they're up there drinking split pea soup and grinning and pointing at the moon and the pier and all the trees. You're both hung up. (*The phone rings off left,* JOY *crosses the stage and exits left.* STU *remains standing and looking off left.*)

JOY
(*Off left*) Hello. How are you, Joe? Sure. Okay. Yes, I got the job. Of course. How about you? Well, pretty soon I guess. Yes, I bought my ticket. Uh-huh. Well, as soon as I can. Yes. Sure. Come on over. Okay. Good. 'Bye. (*She hangs up and comes on from left carrying a fishing pole; she crosses to* STU *and kisses him on the stomach, then exits right.*)

STU
That was Joe, huh? (*He sits.*)

JOY
(*Off right*) Yes. He's coming over.

STU
Good.

MYRA
(*Off right*) Good biscuits, Joy.

JOY
They're all right.

STU
Are you packing, Joy?

JOY
What?

STU
Are you getting your stuff ready?

JOY
Yes.

STU
That's going to be a good trip.

JOY
I guess so.

STU
All that way on a train. The seats fold back so you can sleep if you want to. You can look out the window too. You can see all kinds of different houses and people walking around. (JOE *comes on from left wearing a suit and dark glasses and carrying a fishing pole and a suitcase; he looks at* STU *for a while, then crosses the stage and exits right.*) They have one whole car where you eat. And another car just for drinking. The tables are nailed to the floor so they don't jiggle. You can buy a whole dinner for about five bucks. They even give you a full pitcher of ice water. They just leave it on the table so you don't have to keep asking for water. And a silver cup full of toothpicks. You sit there and pick your teeth and look out the window. Then you have to leave. They force you to leave

because there's a whole line of people waiting to eat.
They're all hungry.

JOY
(*Off right*) Hi, Joe.

JOE
(*Off right*) Hi.

MYRA
(*Off right*) Have a biscuit.

JOE
Thanks.

STU
They stop once in a while but you can only get off at the
big stations. You can only get off at places like St. Louis
or Cincinnati. None of the small towns. And your butt
aches after a while. Your butt really starts to ache. You
can hardly stand it. So you have to get up and walk
around. Up and down the aisles. Back and forth.

JOE
(*Off right*) Hm. Real butter.

JOY
(*Off right*) Yes. It's starting to melt though.

STU
Your butt aches so bad that your legs even start to ache.
Your legs can fall asleep on a train. Then your feet. You
have to walk fast. It's better to sit in the rest room because you can stretch. You can stretch your legs out in
there. And there's old men in there taking nips on little
wine bottles. They get drunk in there and throw up on
the floor. Their wives don't even know it because they're
asleep in the folding chairs.

MYRA
(*Off right*) Delicious.

JOE

(*Off right*) Good jam, too.

STU

Then everyone falls asleep. Almost everyone at once. It's dark so they figure they have to, I guess. The porter turns the lights out and right away everyone's asleep. There's a little girl running up and down the aisle. She doesn't make any noise because everyone's sleeping. There's a Marine making it with somebody's wife because her husband's drunk in the rest room. There's a cowboy picking his teeth and spitting little gobs of food into the aisle. Some fat guy is farting and he doesn't even know it. The smell drifts down the aisle and stinks up the whole car. One fart after another. Big windy farts that sort of make a whizzing sound. Nobody can hear him but it stinks the whole car up. (SALLY *enters from left wearing dark glasses, fur coat, and carrying a suitcase and a fishing pole; she watches* STU *for a while, then crosses to the tub and stands there.*) He moves a little in the seat because he can feel it, I guess. His wife moves a little and rubs her nose. Then they keep on sleeping. The car stinks more and more. The smell gets into the seats and the pillows and the rug. Everyone's smelling it at the same time. They sleep more and more. Then it's morning.

SALLY

Hi.

STU

(*Sitting up and yawning*) Whew! What time is it?

SALLY

Seven.

STU

Are you going, too?

SALLY
Yep.

STU
Do you have all your stuff?

SALLY
Yep.

STU
It's a good day to leave.

SALLY
Why?

STU
I mean it's sunny. The sun's out.

SALLY
It's cold though.

STU
But when the sun's out you don't notice it.

SALLY
I guess. I'm going to eat.

STU
Okay. (*She exits right.*) The water's up. The sun's on the water already. (*He stands and yells off right.*) Hey, everybody! The sun's on the water!

MYRA
(*Off right*) Really?

STU
Yeah. And the tide's up. We should take a swim.

JOY
(*Off right*) It's too early. (STU *puts the towel over his head.*)

STU

(*Talking like an old lady*) Dainty little things. Too early. Too early to swim. Water's too cold. There's a little bitty wind skippin' over the sand. The shells are too sharp for them dainty feet. Tsk, tsk. Got to wear your tennies on account of the shells. (JIM *comes on from left wearing a suit and dark glasses and carrying a suitcase and fishing pole; he watches* STU.) Got to wear a shirty on account of the sun. Can't lay around in the sand on account of your crotch. Smear a lot a' chicken fat on yer tiny fragile legs. Get back in the cabin, girlie! Don't go faintin' on the beach!

JIM

Are you going, Stu?

STU

(*Still old lady*) None a' yer business, sonny! Get away from this beach! Go on! Get off my sand! Get away from the shells! Git! Git!

JIM

Hey Stu. (*He gives* STU *the finger and goes off right.*)

STU

That don't shock me, sonny! I been around. That kind a' smut don't bother no one nowadays. This is the twentieth century, buddy!

MYRA

(*Off right*) Hi, Jim.

JIM

(*Off right*) Hi.

JOY

Are you ready?

JIM

Sure.

STU

You ain't gonna bother nobody nowadays. You're a bunch
a' sissies! A bunch a' pantywaists! Nobody cares about
the likes a' you! No moxy! No spunk! Can't even swim
on account a' the smoke ya' put in your lungs. A bunch a'
fatsoes. A bunch a' faggots prancin' around. Dancin' in
the streets with yer make-up on. Swishin' into yer gay
restaurants! No balls! That's what! No hair on yer
chest!

JOE

(*Off right*) Do you have everything?

MYRA

(*Off right*) I think so.

JIM

Toothpaste?

JOY

Yep.

STU

(*Still old lady*) Anyway the water's up. There won't be
a boat for days. They don't come in when it's high like
this. The tide and all. Boats are chicken, too. Chickens
run boats. A bunch a' cowards. They'll wait for it to calm.
It'll warm up and they'll come in with their sails down
and their nets hangin' over the edge. They'll all be
drinkin' gin and singin' sea songs. They'll all be horny
for the young virgins that walk the beaches in their two-
piece flimsy things. Then they'll come onto the land and
start screwing everything in sight. The boats'll be hung
up for days because everybody's screwing on the beach.
They'll like it more and more. Once they get the taste for
it they won't stop. The boats will be there for months
because everybody's screwing. Nobody wants to go
nowhere because screwing is all they need. Screwing and

screwing. And all those boats just sitting out there with their sails down and their nets hanging and rotting in the sun. Years go by and they're still screwing. Old sailors with bald heads and old virgins with gray hair. The whole beach littered with bodies on top of each other. The boats are sinking! All those rotten boats falling into the ocean. One at a time. They break into bits and crack each other as they go down. One at a time. They sink. Pieces of wood float and wash up onto the beach but nobody cares. Nobody needs boats or wood or sails or nets. There's a whole new crop of corny virgins walking around. Up and down the beach in their two-pieces. Nobody stops. More babies from the virgins. Males and females up and down the beach. No clothes any more. A mound of greasy bodies rolling in sperm and sand sticking to their backs and sand in their hair. Hair growing all over. Down to their feet. Pubic hair without bows or ribbons. (*He talks in normal voice and takes the towel off his head.*) Hair on their toes. Fires! Fires at night. All over the island there's huge fires flaring and they all lie around. They lie there fucking by the fire and picking each other's nose. They lick each other's arms and growl and purr and fart all they want to. They roll around farting and spitting and licking up and down. Long tongues and wet legs. Then they build a house. A big house way up on the side of a hill. It takes a year to build. It's one house with one room and a fire pit in the middle. They all go in and sit on the floor and make rugs. They make rugs because the floor is cold and they don't like the cold. They start weaving and sewing. Big huge heavy rugs with fringe around the edge and diamond shapes in the middle. Orange and red rugs with yellow diamonds. They stop screwing, see, and they just make rugs. All day. Years of making rugs until the whole house is covered. The walls are covered and the ceiling and the floor. The windows are blocked up and they sit. The fire's out because of the rugs. It's warm. They're very warm inside. Sitting. It's dark, see. Pitch black and no sound. Because of the rugs. Then they start to giggle. One of them starts and they all start. One after another until they can't stop. The whole house is giggling. Then they scream, see. They start screaming all together because they can't breathe. On account of the rugs. The rugs are all sewn together and it's very warm. It's boiling hot inside. They start to sweat and run around. They bump into each other because it's dark. They can't see so they hit and claw each other with their nails. They have long nails. They kick and scream and the sweat is rolling off them. They can't breathe and it's hot. They're screaming, see. (*Off stage right the actors giggle,* STU *sits slowly in the bathtub, the giggling stops.*) And they come out. One at a time. They walk in a line out of the house. One behind the other. Down the side of the hill. Through the woods. They don't say anything. They don't even breathe. They just walk in a line. Down to the beach. They walk across the beach and right into the water. One behind the other. They just keep walking until you can't see them any more. (*He lies back in the tub so that his head is out of view and his feet hang over the edge.* JOY *comes on from right dressed in a bright red hat and a red dress; she is pulling a wagon loaded with all the suitcases. The rest of the actors come on whistling and cheering, they all hold their fishing poles, they stand in a group stage right waving and throwing kisses at* JOY *as* JOY *backs up slowly with the wagon waving back to them.*)

MYRA
Have a good time!

SALLY
So long, Joy!

JOE
So long!

JIM
Good luck out there!

JOE
See you, babe!

JIM
'Bye!

JOE
'Bye, 'bye!

JOY
'Bye!

MYRA
Say hello for me!

JOE
Don't forget!

JIM
Have fun!

JOE
Good luck!

JOY
Thanks!

JOE
See you later! (JOY *keeps backing up with the wagon and exits left. The four actors throw kisses, then walk slowly downstage; they stand in a line across the stage facing the audience, then they all cast their lines into the audience. They sit simultaneously and look at the audience while holding their poles.*)

STU

(*With his head still unseen*) Then the water goes out
again because it's nighttime. I guess it goes out. Yes. At
night the water always goes out. And the sand gets all
dry in the place where the water used to be. You can hear
it making little slapping sounds and getting farther
away from the pier. There's a breeze sort of. One of
those high breezes that just hits the top of your head and
blows paper cups down the beach. Your back shivers a
little and you get goose bumps on your legs. Your toes
start to sweat. The sweat runs down between your toes
and your feet swell up and stick to your socks. You can't
move because your feet are stuck. You can't move your
head. Your head stays straight and your eyes are wide
open. You can't blink your eyes. Your hands sweat just
like your feet. Your fingers swell up like your toes. (*The
lights start to dim slowly.*) The sweat runs down your
arms and down your legs. You're looking out and you
can see the water. You can see it in the dark because it's
white. Like milk. The whole top is covered with milk. It
smells. Your nose is burning from the smell but you can't
move. You keep looking to the other side. The smell gets
worse and your ears start to hum. You can see these little
dots on the other side. These lights. Your eyes stay open.
Then you move. You start to move slowly up the beach.
Your feet hurt and your nose is bleeding from the smell.
Then you see the lights again. And they blink. One after
the other. Between the trees. You can see them blinking.
On and off. A whole town. (JOY *backs on stage from left
again pulling the wagon; she exits right.*) Your eyes start
blinking with the lights. Your feet start moving. You
can feel them move inside your socks. Then your arms.
You're running. You can feel the breathing. Panting
sort of. The wind comes in through your nose and dries
the blood. You can taste it. Your mouth opens and the

wind comes in. Your body's moving. The sweat dries on your legs. You're going now. Much faster and the breathing gets harder. You can see the lights better now. Yellow lights between the trees. The smell stops. The humming stops. The lights go out. (*The lights come up to their full brightness,* STU *jumps out of the bathtub and crosses very fast downstage center facing the audience, the other actors remain sitting and staring at the audience.*)

STU

Good! (*He breathes in and out very fast.*) That's great! See my stomach. In and out. It's breathing. I'm taking it in. The air. What a fine bunch of air I'm taking in. Now I'm taking it in through my nose. See. (*He breathes through his nose.*) Aaah! Great! Now my mouth. (*He breathes through his mouth.*) Good! In and out! Ladies and gentlemen, the air is fine! All this neat air gathered before us! It's too much! (*The other actors start to breathe slowly, gradually, making sounds as they inhale and exhale.*) The place is teeming with air. All you do is breathe. Easy. One, two. One, two. In. Out. Out, in. I learned this in fourth grade. Breathing, ladies and gentlemen! Before your very eyes. Outstanding air. All you need to last a day. Two days. A week. Month after month of breathing until you can't stop. Once you get the taste of it. The hang of it. What a gas. In your mouth and out your nose. Ladies and gentlemen, it's fantastic! (*They all breathe in unison as* JOY *backs on stage from right pulling the wagon; she exits slowly left as the lights dim and go out. There are three loud knocks from the back of the house.*)

The End

Icarus's Mother

ICARUS'S MOTHER *was first produced at the Caffe Cino. It was directed by Michael Smith and played by James Barbosa, John Kramer, Cynthia Harris, Lee Worley, and John Coe. It was subsequently produced by David Wheeler at the Theatre Company at Boston.*

NOTES ON *ICARUS'S MOTHER*

I directed the first production of *Icarus's Mother* (premiere: November 16, 1965) at the Caffe Cino in New York. It was Joe Cino's idea. I didn't know Sam Shepard, but I already had a special feeling about his work. His earliest plays, *Cowboys* and *Rock Garden,* had formed the first production of Theatre Genesis a year before. I was dazzled by them—their immediacy and vitality, the freshness and integrity of the author's voice. I wrote a rave review in the *Village Voice* and felt forever after as though I'd "discovered" Sam Shepard.

I immediately liked *Icarus's Mother;* and I still think it is the best of Sam's plays to date—the fullest, densest, most disturbing and provocative. But it is terribly difficult to produce. I failed. Maybe I can share the lessons of that failure.

When I read it, I couldn't tell the characters apart—and Sam said he doesn't think about characters. I was struck by the play's smooth, mysterious ascent from cozy reality to high lyricism and symbolism, its debonair plunge into the sharky deeps of resonant meaning. All Sam's plays use the stage to project images: they do not relate to the spectator by reflecting outside reality (they are not psychological or political) ; rather they relate to reality by operating directly on the spectator's mind and nerves. The imagery is surreal, the method nonrational, the sensibility hunchy. It's always hard to tell what, if anything, Sam's plays are "about"—although they are unmistakably alive. *Icarus's Mother* is exceptionally ambitious, and I think it succeeds in objectifying its impulse, externalizing it in terms of human actions and reactions and stage events.

Icarus's Mother is about fear—specifically, the so-called paranoia of the nuclear present—and its effect on people individually and in community. The plane is a vivid and convincing symbolic threat; its equivocal reality and inexplicable relation to the characters—does it after all have anything to do with them?—are as disorienting as the Bomb it may be thought to carry.

As director I approached the play all wrong. I started rehearsals by talking about its content and overall meaning. Trouble. The actors didn't share my interpretation or even care about it. More important, they couldn't use it: it didn't give them anything to do.

Mistake two—language. The play's basic diction is cool, almost unexpressive; then three times it erupts into huge monologues that overflow its token naturalism. (They are in fact the means by which it transcends itself.) I thought of them as arias and looked for the music of the play. Again I was blocking the actors. Our nexus of anxiety was the smoke signals. "What are we doing?" they'd ask. I told them they were making smoke signals. "Why?" Don't think about that, just do it. "What is the motivation?" I could make things up, but they seemed irrelevant. I figured out how to make smoke, I showed the actors how to hold the blanket, gave them gestures and rhythms and sounds. Not enough. They were confused, uncomfortable, floundering. How could I free them from worry? How could I get them simply to *do* it, not to *act* it? They felt foolish just going through the motions, and the results were self-conscious and hollow.

Tardily we got to work on character, at which the actors were expert. It turned out that the characters in *Icarus's Mother* are perfectly distinct, it's just that we're given almost no information about them. Close scrutiny reveals a coherent pattern of response for each of them, and it's possible to extrapolate backwards from that pattern to postulate the omitted facts. We decided that Howard and Pat are married. She's depressed and he's fed up with it; she's self-indulgent, he's mean. Jill is Bill's girl friend, a warm cheerful girl who does what she can to distract Pat and keep Howard from tormenting her. Bill is an overage Boy Scout, a little dumb, easily scared by his own fantasies. Frank is older, we decided, an envious outsider to the group, charming enough but clumsy. Bill and Howard retreat into boyhood when frightened; they play with their security blanket, try to control reality with symbolic gestures, shut the girls out, try to turn Frank off.

All this fits fine, although a whole different set of hypotheses might be equally good or better. But at last we had something we could work on.

We were at about this stage on opening night, and for the first week the production was terrible—heavy, unconvincing, obscure, forced. Only then did I realize that the play is about a picnic. That should have been my first concern, the picnic, instead of all the probing into meaning, all the theories about paranoia and politics. And at last the play began to come together. The dialogue isn't Sam being arty, it's people talking, people who know each other and don't have to explain themselves, people who are hot and a little bored and a little too full of food. And so on. Lesson: go for the reality. The meaning is built in. Get the reality, and the meaning takes care of itself.

But it's not that simple, and realism isn't all there is to *Icarus's Mother*. It needs reality in order to transcend reality—and it's the transcending that makes the play extraordinary. The smoke signals are just barely possible as real behavior; finally, essentially, they are the abstract gestures of a formal rite. The long speeches really are more operatic than conversational. The plane transforms from everyday artifact into agent of apocalypse behind a veil of fantasy and deception. And how do you go from real plane to planes of reality? I don't know.

Sam Shepard overreaches the boundaries of the known and possible. Who is Icarus? The play itself is Icarus, and if it fails, then so did Icarus fail. Would you have him heed his father's warning?

Michael Smith

SCENE

(*The stage is covered with grass. A low hedge upstage runs the width of the stage. Behind the hedge is a pale blue scrim. Center stage is a portable barbecue with smoke rising out of it. The lighting is bright yellow. On the grass down left is a tablecloth with the remnants of a huge meal scattered around it.* BILL *lies on his back down left staring at the sky.* HOWARD *lies up left,* JILL *up right,* PAT *down right and* FRANK *center stage—all in the same position as* BILL *and staring at the sky. Before the lights come up the sound of birds chirping is heard. The sound lasts for a while. The lights come up very slowly as the sound fades out. The lights come up full. A long pause, then all the people start belching at random. They stop.*)

BILL
(*Still staring at the sky*) Does he know there's people down here watching him do that?

JILL
Sure.

PAT
It's skywriting.

HOWARD
No, it's not skywriting. It's just a trail. A gas trail.

PAT
I thought it was.

FRANK
It's gas.

BILL
I don't like it. I don't like the looks of it from here. It's distracting.

30

FRANK
It's a vapor trail. All jets do it.

BILL
I don't like the way he's making it. I mean a semicircle thing like that. In a moon shape.

JILL
I like it.

BILL
If he knows what he's doing, that means he could be signaling or something.

FRANK
Jets don't signal.

PAT
It's gas, Bill.

BILL
You mean that whole long stream of cloud is just excess gas?

HOWARD
Right.

BILL
He has no other way of getting rid of it?

HOWARD
Nope. (BILL *stands, looking up at the sky.*)

BILL
And he's spreading it all over the sky like that?

HOWARD
That's right.

BILL
He's staying in the same general area, though. How

come he's not moving to some other areas? He's been right above us for the past hour.

FRANK
He's probably a test pilot or something.

BILL
I think he sees us. I don't like the looks of it.

HOWARD
He's a million miles up. How could he see us?

BILL
He sees our smoke and he's trying to signal. (*Yelling at the sky*) Get away from here! Get out of our area! (HOWARD *stands, looking up at the sky.*)

HOWARD
He can't hear you, Bill. You'll have to be louder than that.

BILL
Hey! Get your gas away from here!

FRANK
Sit down.

BILL
We don't know what you want but we don't want you around here!

JILL
He can't hear you. What's the matter with you?

HOWARD
He can see us, though. He knows we're looking at him.

BILL
If you need help you'll have to come down!

HOWARD
(*Yelling at the sky*) We ate all the food so we can't give you any!

FRANK
Sit down, you guys.

BILL
Get away from the picnic area! Go somewhere else! Go on! Get away from the park!

JILL
Will you guys cut it out. Leave the poor guy alone. He's just flying. Let him fly.

HOWARD
He's not just flying. If he were just doing that it would be all right. But he's not. He's signaling.

JILL
Who would he be signaling to?

HOWARD
His mother, maybe. Or his wife.

BILL
He could be signaling to anybody.

FRANK
Not likely.

PAT
What if he is? So what?

BILL
So, someone should be told about it. The community should know.

PAT
Let him signal his wife if he wants to. He's probably been away for a while and he just got back. Let him show off a little.

HOWARD
But he's right above us. His wife isn't down here.

JILL
I'm his wife.

BILL
Are you his wife, Jill?

JILL
That's right.

BILL
Then we should tell him, so he doesn't have to waste any more time.

HOWARD
Come on down! Your wife's down here!

BILL
Come on down here! (JILL *stands and yells at the sky.*)

JILL
Come here, honey! Here I am! (*She waves.*)

BILL
Come and get her! (FRANK *stands and yells at the sky.*)

FRANK
Come and get your wife, stupid! (*The following lines should happen on top of each other, with whistling and ad-lib shouts from all the actors.*)

HOWARD
Come on! Land that thing!

JILL
Here I am, sweetheart! (*Throwing kisses*)

FRANK
You'd better hurry! (PAT *stands and yells at the sky.*)

PAT
Come on down! Here we are! Yoo hoo!

BILL
Your other wife's here, too!

FRANK
Two wives!

PAT
Come on, sweetie! Where have you been!

JILL
We've been waiting and waiting!

FRANK
Two ripe juicy wives waiting for you!

HOWARD
Come on!

BILL
You've been up there too long, mister!

FRANK
We can see you! Come on down!

BILL
Land that thing!

PAT
Come to me, booby! Boobsy, boobsy, boobsy. (JILL *and*
PAT *start shimmying around the stage.*)

HOWARD
We've got your wives, mister pilot! You'd better come
down or we'll take them away!

BILL
We'll use them ourselves! There's three of us here!

FRANK
He's leaving! Look! Hey!

HOWARD
Hey don't! Come back here!

JILL
He's leaving us! Stop!

PAT
Darling! The children!

BILL
You're running out on your kids! (*They all yell and shake their fists at the sky.*)

JILL
Don't leave us! Come back here!

HOWARD
You're no good, mister pilot!

PAT
Come back! The children!

JILL
Don't leave us, darling! (*They all boo loudly.*)

BILL
What a rotten guy! (*They stop booing and just stare at the sky.*)

FRANK
He's gone.

HOWARD
That makes me sick. (*A pause as they all stare at the sky*)

PAT
Well, when do they start this thing?

FRANK
Are you in a hurry?

PAT

No. I just want to know so I could take a walk or something in the meantime.

BILL

They don't start till it gets dark.

FRANK

Where are you going to walk to?

PAT

Just down the beach or something. To rest my stomach. That was a big meal, you know.

FRANK

Walking doesn't rest your stomach. When you're full and you walk, that just irritates it.

JILL

He's right.

PAT

All right! I'll walk just to loosen my legs up or something. I'm not going to lie around here waiting for it to get dark, though.

HOWARD

What happens if they start while you're on your walk?

JILL

That'd be terrible, Pat.

PAT

They shoot them in the sky. I can watch fireworks while I'm walking just as easy. It isn't hard. All I have to do is tilt my head up and watch and continue walking.

BILL

You may trip, though, and there you'd be unconscious on the beach somewhere and we'd have to go looking for you.

JILL
Yeah.

HOWARD
Then we'd miss the fireworks just on account of you, Pat.

FRANK
We'd be looking all over. Through the bushes and up and down the beach for hours. Everyone would miss everything.

JILL
Then maybe someone else would trip while they were looking for you and we'd have two missing people on the beach unconscious instead of just one.

BILL
We might all trip and be there on the beach for weeks unconscious.

PAT
All right! (*She sits; the rest remain standing and close in on her, slowly forming a circle.*)

HOWARD
You can walk if you want to, Pat. While it's still light. We don't mind.

JILL
We don't want to wreck your fun, Patsy.

BILL
But you have to get back before it gets dark. Because that's when the fireworks start. And you don't want to miss them.

FRANK
You don't want to be lost on the beach by yourself and suddenly hear loud booming sounds and suddenly see the sky all lit up with orange and yellow and blue and green

and purple and gold and silver lights. (*They gather around* PAT *in a circle, looking down at her as she remains seated.*)

JILL
That'd be scary.

HOWARD
You might run and fall and scream. You might run right into the ocean and drown or run right into the forest.

BILL
They'd have to send helicopters out looking for you.

JILL
Or jets.

BILL
Your husband in the jet would find you. (PAT *stands suddenly.*)

PAT
Shut up! I don't have a husband in a jet and neither does Jill! So stop kidding around! If I want to walk, I will! Just to walk! Just to walk down the beach and not come back till after dark. To loosen my legs up after a big dinner like that.

FRANK
We were just kidding, Pat. (*They all sit slowly around Pat.*)

PAT
Boy! That's something. Trying to scare me into not walking. What a group.

FRANK
We were kidding.

PAT
Shut up, Frank! Jesus. All of a sudden picnics are local-

ized events. We all have to hang around the same area where we eat. We can't even walk. We eat a big steak and we can't walk it off. (HOWARD *stands and grabs* PAT'S *hand; he starts pulling her stage left.*)

HOWARD
Let's walk! Come on, Pat. Here we go walking. Where do you want to walk to? (*The rest remain seated.*)

PAT
Cut it out! Let go! Let go of my hand! (*He holds her hand tightly, staring at her.*)

HOWARD
I would like very much to take a walk. You're absolutely right about the steak. We need to walk it off.

PAT
Let go, Howard, or I'll kick you.

BILL
Let her go, Howard.

HOWARD
But she's right. We should all walk after steak dinners. The stomach works best when the whole body's in motion. All the acid gets sloshed around. (PAT *struggles violently to get away,* HOWARD *grabs her other arm and holds her tightly, they face each other.*)

PAT
Let me go! Let go of my arm, Howard! I'll kick you. I really will.

FRANK
Come on. Let her go.

HOWARD
But she's right, Frank.

FRANK
Her husband may come back in his jet plane and see what
you're doing. Then you'll be in trouble.

PAT
Very funny.

BILL
He might.

JILL
Then he'll land and do you in with a ray gun or a laser
beam.

HOWARD
But we'll be way up the beach. Jets can't land on a little
strip of beach. We'll be under some bushes even. He won't
even see us. Will he, Pat? (*He shakes her.*) Will he, Pat?

PAT
He might.

JILL
See?

HOWARD
Pat's lying, though. Jets fly at an altitude of approximately five thousand feet and move at a minimum of
approximately five hundred miles an hour with an air
velocity of approximately—and a wind velocity and the
pilot can't even hear or see or anything. He's just hung
in space and he can't hear or see. Can he, Pat? (*He shakes*
PAT *more violently.* PAT *gives no resistance.*) Can he or
can't he? No he can't! Oh yes he can! He can see fireworks because fireworks explode at an altitude of approximately five hundred feet and give off powerful light
rays and make swell patterns in the blue sky right under
his keen old plane! Right? Beautiful. Just think how

beautiful, Pat. We'll be down here on the grass and he'll be way, way, way up in the air. And somewhere in between the two of us there'll be a beautiful display of flashing fireworks. I can hardly wait for nighttime. (*He lets go of* PAT. *She moves downstage slowly, then turns and walks slowly upstage; she stands upstage staring at the scrim.* HOWARD *and the others watch her.*)

HOWARD

Of course you have to let yourself go into aeronautics gradually, Pat. You can't expect to grasp the sensation immediately. Especially if you've never been up before. I mean in anything bigger than a Piper Cub or a Beachcraft Bonanza. Single- or double-propeller jobs of that variety usually don't get you beyond say a sore ear or two sore ears from the buzzing they make. The booming of a jet is something quite different.

JILL

She knows that.

HOWARD

Of course the sound isn't all of the problem. Not at all. It's something about being in the cockpit surrounded by glass and knowing that glass is solid, yet it's something you can see through at the same time. That's the feeling. You know what I mean, Pat? Looking through this glass enclosure at miles and miles of geometric cow pastures and lakes and rivers. Looking through and seeing miles and miles of sky that changes color from gray to blue, then back to gray again as you move through it. There's something to look at all around you. Everywhere you turn in the cockpit you have something to see. You have so much to see that you want to be able to stop the plane and just stay in the same position for about half an hour looking all around you. Just turning your seat from one

42

position to the other until you take it all in. Even then you get the feeling that you'd like to spend more than just half an hour. Maybe a whole hour or two hours or maybe a whole day in that very same position. Just gazing from one side to the other. (*He crosses up to* PAT *slowly and stands behind her.*) Then up, then down. Then all the way around until you realize you don't have enough eyes for that. That maybe if you had a few more eyes you could do that but not with just two. Then you get kind of dizzy and sick to the tum tum and your head starts to spin so you clutch the seat with both hands and close your eyes. But even inside your closed eyes you can see the same thing as before. Miles and miles of cow pasture and city and town. Like a movie. Lake after lake with river after river running away from the lake and going to the ocean. House after house turning into city after city and town after town. So you quick open your eyes and try to fix them on the control panel. You concentrate on the controls and the dials and the numbers. You run your hands over the buttons and the circles and the squares. You can't look up now or around or from side to side or down. You're straight in front straining not to see with peripheral vision. Out of the sides of your eyes like a bird does but straight ahead. But the sky creeps in out of the corner of each eye and you can't help but see. You can't help but want to look. You can't resist watching it for a second or two or a minute. For just a little bitty while. (JILL *stands.*)

JILL
All right! Leave her alone!

HOWARD
Sorry. (*He crosses back down left and sits;* JILL *crosses up to* PAT *and stands beside her, patting her on the back.*)

JILL

We're all going to see the fireworks together. So there's no point in getting everyone all excited. Pat's going to see them with us and nobody's going to walk anywhere.

FRANK

Oh, thanks a lot. (*He stands;* BILL *and* HOWARD *remain sitting.*) Thanks for the consideration, Jill. My stomach happens to be killing me. I could use a walk. And besides I'd like to see the beach.

BILL

We can walk later. After the fireworks.

FRANK

I can't wait and besides I have to pee too. I really do.

JILL

Well go ahead.

HOWARD

Pee here.

FRANK

No!

HOWARD

Pee in your pants.

FRANK .

Look, Howard—

BILL

You can pee in front of us, Frank. It's all right. Pee your heart out.

HOWARD

We don't mind. Really. We're all friends.

JILL

We'll close our eyes, Frank.

44

FRANK
I would like very much to take a nice little walk and pee
by myself, alone. Just for the enjoyment of peeing alone.

BILL
Well go ahead.

FRANK
Thank you. (FRANK *goes off right.*)

HOWARD
How's the girl?

JILL
She's all right. All she needs is some rest.

BILL
Listen, Pat, why don't you and Jill go up the beach with
Frank and pee together under the bushes?

HOWARD
And we'll stay and wait for it to get dark. (*At this point
the lights start to fade, almost imperceptibly, to the end
of the play.*)

BILL
Pat?

HOWARD
We'll wait here, Pat, and save you a place. We'll save all
of you a place to sit.

BILL
How does that sound, Patricia?

HOWARD
It would give you time to rest and settle your stomach
and empty your bladder and loosen your legs. What do
you think?

BILL

You could take as much time as you wanted.

HOWARD

You could even miss the display altogether if you want to do that. I mean it's not mandatory that you watch it. It's sort of a hoax, if you really want to know the truth. I mean if it's anything at all like the one they had last year.

BILL

Last year's was a joke.

HOWARD

That's right, Pat. Most of them didn't even work. The city spent thirty thousand dollars for twenty-five hundred fireworks last year and fifteen hundred of them exploded before they even got off the launching pad. They just made a little pop, and a stream of smoke came out, and that was it. A joke.

JILL

Some of them were beautiful.

BILL

Some of them *were* beautiful. The big gold and silver ones with sparklers on the ends. Then they had rocket ones that went way up and disappeared and then exploded way out over the ocean. They'd change into different colors. First orange, then blue, then bright yellow. Then this little parachute came floating down very softly with a tiny silver light on it. We just watched it slowly falling through the air hanging from the parachute. It went way out and finally sank into the water and the light went out. Then they'd shoot another one.

PAT

(*Still facing upstage*) I'm not going to miss the display. I've seen every one of them for the past ten years and I'm not going to miss this one.

JILL

Of course not, Pat. (*She strokes her hair.*)

PAT

They get better and better as the years go by. It's true that some of them didn't work last year and that the city got gypped by the firecracker company. But that doesn't mean it will happen again this year. Besides, as Bill said, some of them were beautiful. It's worth it just to see one beautiful one out of all the duds. If none of them work except just one, it will be worth it to see just that one beautiful flashing thing across the whole sky. I'll wait all night on my back, even if they have to go through the whole stack without one of them working. Even if it's the very, very last one in the whole pile and everybody who came to see them left and went home. Even if I'm the only one left in the whole park and even if all the men who launch the firecrackers go home in despair and anguish and humiliation. I'll go down there myself and hook up the thing by myself and fire the thing without any help and run back up here and lie on my back and wait and listen and watch the goddam thing explode all over the sky and watch it change colors and make all its sounds and do all the things that a firecracker's supposed to do. Then I'll watch it fizzle out and I'll get up slowly and brush the grass off my legs and walk back home and all the people will say what a lucky girl. What a lucky, lucky girl.

JILL

We'll see them, Patty. Don't worry.

BILL

Jill, why don't you take Pat up the beach for a little walk? We'll wait for you. It would do you both good.

JILL

Do you want to walk, Patty?

PAT

Will we be back in time?

JILL

Sure. We'll just take a short walk and come right back. (PAT *turns downstage.*)

PAT

All right. But just a short one.

BILL

That's a girl. (JILL *leads* PAT *by the arm; they go off right.*)

HOWARD

Take your time and we'll save your places. (BILL *and* HOWARD *look at each other for a second, then they both get up and cross to the barbecue.* HOWARD *picks up the tablecloth and drapes it over the barbecue,* BILL *holds one side of the tablecloth while* HOWARD *holds the other, they look up at the sky, then they lift the tablecloth off the barbecue and allow some smoke to rise; they replace the tablecloth over the barbecue and follow the same procedure, glancing up at the sky; they do this three or four times, then* FRANK *enters from left in bare feet and carrying his shoes.*)

FRANK

What a beach! (HOWARD *and* BILL *turn suddenly to* FRANK *and drop the tablecloth on the ground.*) It's fantastic! The beach is fantastic, you guys. (*They just stare at* FRANK.) You ought to go down there. No beer cans, no seaweed, no nothing. Just beach and water and a few rocks. It's out of the question. We ought to go down there and sit. That'd be the place to watch fireworks from. Right on the sand. We could move our stuff down there. What about it?

HOWARD
There's flak and little particles that fly off in those explosions. It gets in your eyes.

FRANK
Well it would get in our eyes up here just as easy.

HOWARD
Not likely. We're above sea level here.

FRANK
So what?

HOWARD
So the air is denser above sea level and the flak and shrapnel and—well it's just safer up here. Besides there's waves to contend with at sea level. And there's sand and we're away from the smell up here. There's a nice little breeze up here.

FRANK
I'd like to be down there myself. (*He crosses upstage and stares over the hedge as though looking down at a beach.*)

BILL
Why don't you go.

FRANK
I'd like to. It'd be nice lying there with the waves right next to me and explosions in the air.

HOWARD
Go ahead, Frank. We'll stay here.

FRANK
Well we could all go. Like an expedition or an exploration. We could all find out what there is to know about the beach before it gets dark.

BILL
There's nothing to know. The beach is composed of sand

which is a product of the decomposition of rock through the process of erosion. Sand is the residue of this decomposition which, through the action and movement of tides controlled by the location of the moon in relation to the position of the other planets in the hemisphere, finds itself accumulating in areas which are known to us as beaches.

FRANK
But it stretches so far out. It'd be nice to walk to the end of it and then walk back.

HOWARD
Go, then! Nobody's stopping you! Have fun! Go roll around in it. (FRANK *turns downstáge.*)

FRANK
Boy! You guys are really something. It interests me to know that I've been living in this community for ten years and never knew about this beach. I mean I never knew it was so clean. I expected trash all over and a huge stench from dead fish. But instead I find a long old beach that seems to go out to some kind of a peninsula or something. That's nice to see. I'd like to try hiking out there some day. That's an interesting thing to know. That you could spend a day hiking with a nice group of friendly neighborly neighbors and pack a lunch and make a weekend of it even. Or maybe two weekends' worth, depending on the weather and the friendliness of the neighbors and the cost of the baby sitters involved.

BILL
That sounds very nice, Frank.

FRANK
I think so.

BILL
We'll have to try that.

FRANK
Where are the girls?

HOWARD
They left. They said they were going to go look for you.

BILL
They wanted to tell you something.

FRANK
What?

BILL
They wouldn't say. Something important.

FRANK
They're just kidding. (*He crosses down left.*)

HOWARD
No. It was something big, though, because they wouldn't tell us even. We asked them what it was and they said they could only tell you.

FRANK
Something big?

HOWARD
Some kind of secret.

FRANK
Did they giggle about it?

BILL
Yeah but they wouldn't tell. We even threatened them. We told them we'd take them home before the fireworks started if they didn't tell. (FRANK *crosses down right.*)

FRANK
And they still didn't tell?

BILL
Nope. Something exciting, they said.

FRANK
But they giggled a lot?

BILL
Yep.

FRANK
I bet I know what it is.

HOWARD
You do?

FRANK
If it's what I think it is I'll kill both of them. Do you want to know what I think it is?

HOWARD
No. They said it was top secret. We don't want to know until you find out first.

FRANK
Well I already know.

HOWARD
Not for sure. Go find out for sure, then come back and tell us.

FRANK
Okay, but it's really a joke if it's what I think it is. And if it is what I think it is they're going to be in real trouble.

HOWARD
Go find out.

FRANK
Which way did they go? (HOWARD *and* BILL *both point off right.*)

FRANK
Thanks a lot. I'll see you later. (*He goes off right.*)

Icarus's Mother

BILL

Good luck. (BILL *and* HOWARD *pick up the tablecloth and drape it over the barbecue again; they look up at the sky, then lift the tablecloth. They do this a couple of times, then* JILL *and* PAT *enter from left, laughing hysterically and slapping each other on the back; they are in bare feet and carry their shoes.* BILL *and* HOWARD *drop the tablecloth and turn to the girls.*)

JILL

Too much! What a nut! (*They both double over with laughter as* BILL *and* HOWARD *watch them.* PAT *falls on the ground and rolls around, laughing and holding her sides;* JILL *stands over her.*)

PAT

Oh my side!

JILL

Do you know—do you know what this idiot did? Do you know what she did! She—we're walking up the beach, see— we're walking along like this. (*She walks very slowly with her head down.*) Very slowly and dejected and sad. So suddenly she stops. We both stop and she says, guess what? And I said what? She says I really do—I really do have to pee after all. (*They both break up.*) So I said all right. I'm very serious with her, see. I say all right, Patsy dear, if you have to you have to. So then she said I have to pee so bad I can't even wait. I have to go right now. Right this very minute. So we're in the middle of the beach with nothing around but sand. No bushes or nothing. So she whips down her pants and crouches right there in the middle of the beach very seriously. And I'm standing there looking around. Sort of standing guard. And do you know what happens? (*They crack up.*) All of a sudden I have to pee too. I mean

53

really bad like she has to. So I whip my pants down and crouch down right beside her. There we are sitting side by side on the beach together. (*She crouches down in the position.*) Like a couple of desert nomads or something. So. You know how it is when you have to pee so bad that you can't pee at all? (BILL *and* HOWARD *nod their heads.*) Well that's what happened. Neither one of us could get anything out and we were straining and groaning and along comes our friend in the jet plane. Except this time he's very low. Right above our heads. Zoom! So there we were. We couldn't stand up because then he'd really see us. And we couldn't run because there was nowhere to run to. So we just sat and pretended we were playing with shells or something. But he kept it up. He kept flying back and forth right above our heads. So do you know what this nut does? (HOWARD *and* BILL *shake their heads.*) She starts waving to him and throwing kisses. Then he really went nuts. He started doing flips and slides with that jet like you've never seen before. (*She stands with her arms outstretched like a plane.*) He went way up and then dropped like a seagull or something. We thought he was going to crash even. Then I started waving and the guy went insane. He flew that thing upside down and backwards and every way you could imagine. And we were cracking up all over the place. We started rolling in the sand and showing him our legs. Then we did some of those nasty dances like they do in the bars. Then we both went nuts or something and we took off our pants and ran right into the water yelling and screaming and waving at his plane.

PAT

(*Lying on her back and staring at the sky.*) Then he did a beautiful thing. He started to climb. And he went way, way up about twenty thousand feet or forty thousand feet. And he wrote this big sentence across the sky with his vapor trail. He wrote "E equals MC squared" in huge letters. It was really nice.

BILL
Are you sure he saw you?

JILL
Well he wasn't doing all those tricks for nothing.

BILL
But are you sure it was the same guy?

JILL
Of course.

HOWARD
It couldn't have been anyone else?

JILL
Not a chance.

HOWARD
Because Frank told us that guy crashed. (PAT *stands suddenly.*)

PAT
What?

HOWARD
He said that he saw that very same jet go down in the middle of the ocean.

PAT
When?

HOWARD
Just before you came back.

JILL
So where did Frank go?

BILL

To get some help. They're trying to fish him out right now.

PAT

You mean he crashed into the water?

BILL

That's what he told us. It could be a different guy, though.

JILL

I doubt it.

HOWARD

The plane exploded just before it hit the water.

PAT

No!

BILL

That's what Frank said.

JILL

Well let's try to find him, Pat.

BILL

He went that way. (*He points off right.*)

PAT

Aren't you guys coming?

HOWARD

We'll wait here.

JILL

Come on, Pat. (*She pulls* PAT *by the arm, they go off right.* HOWARD *and* BILL *pause to look at the sky, then grab the tablecloth quickly; they are about to drape it over the barbecue when* FRANK *enters slowly from left. He seems to wander around the stage undeliberately and staring blankly in front of him.* HOWARD *and* BILL *drop the tablecloth and watch* FRANK.)

HOWARD

Frank? (*Frank continues to walk as he speaks; he moves all over the stage in a daze as* HOWARD *and* BILL *watch.*)

FRANK

Boy, oh boy, oh boy, oh boy. You guys. You guys have missed the fireworks altogether. You should have seen —this is something to behold, this is. This is the nineteenth wonder of the Western, international world brought to you by Nabisco Cracker Corporation for the preservation of historians to come and for historians to go by. This is. If only the weather and the atmospheric conditions had been better than they were it would have beaten the Hindenburg by far more than it did. (*The lights by this time have become very dim, so that the scrim takes on a translucent quality.*) By that I mean to say a recognized world tragedy of the greatest proportion and exhilaration to make the backs of the very bravest shudder with cold sensations and the hands moisten with the thickest sweat ever before known, ever. And the eyes to blink in disbelief and the temples swell with pounds and the nose run with thick sticky pus. Oh you guys should have come, you guys should have. What a light! (*There is a tremendous boom off stage, followed in a few seconds by flashes of light on stage changing from orange to blue to yellow and then returning to the dim lighting of before; the flashes should come from directly above them. This all occurs while* FRANK *continues, oblivious to everything but what he's saying;* HOWARD *and* BILL *remain in their positions.*) And to happen while walking head down looking at your toes and counting your steps. To happen under private conditions on sand. To be thinking about killing your baby boy or your baby girl or your wife or your wife's sister or your pet dog. And to come to a standstill. (*Another boom followed by the same lighting and returning to the dim; the sound of a vast crowd of people starts faintly and builds in volume to the end of the play.*) To stop still in your tracks, thinking about the night to come and how long it takes to build a beach given the right amount of sand and the right amount of time and the right amount of water to push everything up. Bigger bodies of water with more rain and less sun. More water than land ever. In volume, in density, in the stratospheric conditions. And to hear a sound so shrieking that it ain't even a sound at all but goes beyond that into the inside of the center of each ear and rattles you up so you don't know exactly or for sure if you'll ever hear again or if it actually exactly matters. And it pulls your head straight up off your shoulders in a straight line with the parallel lines of each leg and so each tendon leading to your jawbone strains to its utmost. (*Another boom followed by the lighting; the crowd increases.*) So your eyes bob back and roll around in their sockets and you see the silver-sleek jet, streamlined for speed, turn itself upside down and lie on its back and swoop up, then give itself in so it looks like it's floating. Then another boom and it falls head down just gliding under its own weight. Passing cloud after cloud and picking up its own speed under its own momentum, out of control. Under its own force, falling straight down and passing through flocks of geese on their way back from where they came from. Going beyond itself with the pilot screaming and the clouds breaking up. (*Another boom and light*) And the windows cracking and the wings tearing off. Going through seagulls now, it's so close. Heading straight for the top of the flat blue water. Almost touching in slow motion and blowing itself up six inches above sea level to the dismay of ducks bobbing along. And lighting up the air with a gold tint and a yellow tint and smacking the water so that waves go up to five hundred feet in silver white and blue. Exploding the water for a hundred miles in diameter around itself. Sending a wake to Japan. An eruption of froth and smoke and flame blowing itself up over and over again. Going on and on till the community comes out to see for itself. (*Another boom and light*) Till the houses open because of the light, they can't sleep. And the booming goes on. And the porches are filled with kids in pajamas on top of their fathers shielding their eyes. And their mothers hold their fathers with their mouths open and the light pouring in and their cats running for cover. (*The booming sounds come closer together now and the lighting keeps up a perpetual change from color to color in bright flashes; the crowd noise gets very loud.* FRANK *moves faster around the stage, almost shouting the lines;* HOWARD *and* BILL *hold hands and stand very close together.*) And the sound keeps up and the doors open farther and farther back into the city. And the whole sky is lit. The sirens come and the screaming starts. The kids climb down and run to the beach with their mothers chasing and their fathers chasing them. Oh what a sight to see with your very own eyes. How lucky to be the first one there! And the tide breaks open and the waves go up!

BILL
Stop it, Frank!

FRANK
The water goes up to fifteen hundred feet and smashes the trees, and the firemen come. The beach sinks below the surface. The seagulls drown in flocks of ten thousand. There's a line of people two hundred deep. Standing in line to watch the display. And the pilot bobbing in the very center of a ring of fire that's closing in. His white helmet bobbing up and bobbing down. His hand reaching for his other hand and the fire moves in and covers him

up and the line of two hundred bow their heads and moan together with the light in their faces. Oh you guys should have come! You guys should have been there! You guys— (*He staggers off left.* HOWARD *and* BILL *stand very still, facing out to the audience and holding hands.* JILL *rushes on from right.*)

JILL
Come on, you guys! The plane went down. Come and look! Come on!

HOWARD
Get away from here!

JILL
Everybody's down there! It's fantastic. The plane crashed, Bill! It really did!

BILL
Get away from the picnic area!

JILL
All right. But you guys are missing out. (*She runs off right,* HOWARD *and* BILL *stand very still, the crowd noise becomes deafening, the lights dim slowly out, the sound stops.*)

The End

Fourteen Hundred Thousand

FOURTEEN HUNDRED THOUSAND *was first produced at the Firehouse Theatre, Minneapolis, under the auspices of the Office of Aid to Drama Research at the University of Minnesota. It was directed by Sydney Schubert Walter and played by Steve Friedman, Antoinette Maher, Raymond Henry Stadum, Greta Giving, and David Burns. It was subsequently produced on National Educational Television.*

NOTES ON
FOURTEEN HUNDRED THOUSAND

If the initial production of *Fourteen Hundred Thousand* was in any way a success, it was only in demonstrating to both myself and Sam Shepard some pitfalls that can be encountered when director and playwright work together. From a critical point of view the production was undeniably a failure.

Fourteen Hundred Thousand is a script characterized by an emphasis on language and a highly formal structure. It is true that the dialogue is elliptical, diffuse; that the play is composed of oddly dissimilar fragments joined together without apparent transitions. This diffuse dialogue, however, these strange fragments, are carefully arranged into a precise pattern. The formality is even carried out in the severe lines and deliberate balance of the set, and in the stage directions. These indicate precisely balanced arrangements of characters which emphasize the isolation of one from another. As the play progresses, words become more important, action less important, until it culminates in a technical description read from a book.

Before rehearsals began I made the following decisions independent of the author:

1. I would use a less severe set, one offering possibilities for more dynamic staging.

2. I would ignore the author's stage directions to work for a more casual, naturalistic quality in the opening scenes.

3. As the script became more concentrated on language, as the characters approached a stasis, I would use the actors in an expressionistic way, so that they

conveyed, vocally and physically, the tensions that I felt lay beneath the words.

When Mr. Shepard arrived and rehearsals began, I discovered that all these ideas were unacceptable to him. I had chosen to counter the qualities of the script with the qualities of the production; he wished the production to underline the qualities of the script. The rehearsal period involved a series of compromises which stranded the play in an untheatrical area somewhere between the author's concept and my own. I felt that if Mr. Shepard's ideas for production were followed through, the result would be untheatrical. He felt that my ideas subverted the play's intention.

Fourteen Hundred Thousand is a rich and provocative script, and I feel certain that the right production concept will result in a moving theatrical event. I hope some director will accept the challenge which this play offers.

Sydney Schubert Walter

SCENE

(*A white wall upstage running the width of the stage. A door in the wall stage left. A large bookcase stands from floor to ceiling stage right up against the wall. There are no books in it and it looks as though it's in the process of being built. Sawdust, nails, pieces of wood, saws, etc., are scattered around the floor.* TOM *stands on a stool in front of the bookcase with a hammer in his hand and nails in his mouth. He wears no shirt and is sweating a great deal.* ED *stands in the doorway with the door half open, talking to* TOM, *whose back is to the audience. The lights come up fast to bright blue.*)

ED
The leaves change color now so it looks even more protected than it really is. Vacant is better. No, protected. Something like that. Come up anyway if you get a chance. (ED *shuts the door behind him and exits, the lights change very fast to white, one of the shelves falls off the bookcase onto the floor,* TOM *looks at the shelf for a while, then climbs down off the stool, picks up the shelf, and climbs back up; he replaces the shelf in its former position, the lights change back to blue, the door opens, and* ED *re-enters carrying some lumber, sets the lumber on the floor downstage center.*)

TOM
(*With his back to* ED) This is a rented cabin or something?

ED
No.

TOM
You bought it?

ED

No. It was given to me, donated to me. It's mine to use. One full room. I have to fix it, though. It needs patching, plumbing, electricity, etcetera.

TOM

That's nice of them. (*He hammers a nail into one of the shelves.*)

ED

(*Yelling to be heard over the hammering*) Nice of who? (TOM *stops hammering.*)

TOM

What? Oh—nice of whoever gave it to you. (TOM *starts hammering again.*)

ED

(*Yelling*) Not so nice! I mean they didn't even give it that much thought one way or the other! They weren't really trying to be nice at all. Like I said, it was more in the spirit of a donation! (ED *sits on the lumber with his back to the audience.*)

TOM

(*Looking at the bookcase; he stops hammering.*) That's even nice, though. They didn't have to be necessarily aware of the niceness of what they were doing. In fact if they had been it would have made it anything *but* nice. It would have gone into the realm of charity. I mean the spirit of charity. But they gave it out of no particular spirit at all. It was devoid of any spirit whatsoever, which makes it beautiful and free from emotional claptrap. (TOM *hammers loudly for a while as* ED *looks up at him.*)

ED

(*Yelling*) Anyway it's a full room if you want to come

65

up! Bring a sleeping bag or something! Take the train and come when you can! (TOM *stops hammering.*)

TOM
(*Still staring at the bookcase*) You're going to walk out on me. Is that it? Right in the middle of a job.

ED
Look, I got the structure built for you. You can put in the shelves yourself.

TOM
Thanks, friend.

ED
I have to finish the cabin before it snows. (ED *stands as though to leave.*)

TOM
(*Without turning*) And it does snow up there! Boy, oh boy, the way it can snow when it wants to. A little tiny, eety, beety, teeny, weeny cabin like yours in the midst of a raging blizzard. In the midst of hail and snow and sleet. Calling out for some insulation. Calling for someone to warm its little hearth and seal up its cracking paint. Run to its side before it's too late! Run to its aid and attention! (*A shelf falls off the bookcase onto the floor, the lights change to white, they both stare at the shelf;* DONNA *enters carrying two cans of white paint and two brushes, she kicks the door shut and smiles at* TOM *and* ED.)

DONNA
Hello there and I got some paint. Isn't that fine? So we'll paint it all up between the three of us. (*She sets the cans downstage left on top of each other and sits on them with her back to the audience,* TOM *climbs down off the stool, picks up the shelf, climbs back up, and replaces the shelf.*)

66

TOM

Ed was just thinking about us going to his cabin in the woods. (ED *sits back down on the lumber.*)

DONNA

Seems to me as though that's a bad idea offhand. Bad for several reasons. Bad because we're meeting people, bad because we're building shelves, and bad because we have to paint them. Of course it's good for Ed, however. It could be good for us too if we didn't have so many strikes against us already.

TOM

It's an idea that we had tossed haphazardly into the air without considering all the strikes against us or pondering it for long periods of time.

DONNA

Well. (*She stands and slaps her thigh, she crosses to the bookcase.*) How's it coming?

ED

Tom thinks it could be finished in short order. Seeing as how the frame is all finished, the rest should be easy.

DONNA

Good boy! (*She slaps* TOM *on the butt.*)

ED

The thing is I can't wait around for the grand finale. I have to leave.

DONNA

Oh, it won't be anything to see, Ed. It's just a functional piece of basic furniture for around the house. For everyday use, so to speak.

TOM

Everyday. Everyday nothing. Once! It will be put to use

once in its lifetime and that'll be the end. You never read the books to begin with. The ones you did read you read halfway. The rest you bought for their color or thickness or just to fill up some space. Fourteen hundred thousand books to put in a bookcase once and never touch them again till the day you die.

DONNA
I read like a fool, Tom. You know that and yet you'd like Ed to believe otherwise. In fact you'd like him to believe the exact opposite which is a lie. I could even prove it if it came to a matter of my having to defend my knowledge of books. Would you like me to prove it?

ED
No.

TOM
I don't really care actually. It just seems that books read once are better off in the trash can than they are sitting around on dusty shelves. That's a personal point of view.

ED
Not really. At times I've found myself very briefly getting very attached to books. Very emotionally attached. Like you would with a pet dog. It becomes something that's very hard to give up. You can't just throw it in the garbage with any kind of ease.

TOM
You throw away the book, not the effect. The response of the book stays with you wherever you go, whatever you do. In sickness and in health and through the long sad wintertime. (*He starts hammering;* DONNA *yells.*)

DONNA
We're not going on no vacation until this gets done! Until it's nailed, sanded and painted, and stacked with

68

books on every shelf! Then it's waxed, polished, and smells like the great outdoors! After that then we go! Not before or in the middle! (TOM *stops hammering, the lights change to blue.*)

TOM

It's an impossibility. We'll be here forever. The winter will pass without a vacation, without a change of scenery. There'll be no free moments to wander around through yellow fields or climb purple trees. The task will last forever. (*The door opens very slowly and* MOM *enters with her arms full of books, the other three watch her as she slowly crosses downstage right and stacks the books in a pile on the floor, she sits on the books with her back to the audience;* DONNA *sits on the cans of paint, all three of them look up at* TOM, *who turns around now on the stool to see them.*)

MOM

Whew! It's such a long ways up. It's like climbing three or four mountains in succession. It's also very much like rowing a rowboat in a rowboat race or running many miles over rough terrain in the freezing coldness. My goodness. Dearie.

TOM

I'm not on display, you know.

DONNA

(*Still sitting*) Hi, Mom. I see you brought up some of the books for me. Thanks.

MOM

Yes. A few. They made it very much tougher on me. They must weigh a great deal nowadays. They've changed weight since I was a schoolgirl in my schooling days.

69

TOM

I'm not up here for my health, you know. I have a job
to do.

DONNA

It's worth it though, Mom. When they're all stacked in
and divided into topical categories, it's really a sight
to see.

MOM

Oh indeed. Libraries fascinate me to death. Like ancient
tapestry or Chinese urns or butterfly collections that
I've seen in the past. Many times. Goodness yes.

TOM

This is not a show! I happen not to be a professional
carpenter or an expert nailing person. There's no reason
to watch me work.

ED

It's not you in particular. It's what you're making.

TOM

But *I'm* making it! You're watching *me* make *it!*

MOM

Should we leave here?

DONNA

No, no, no.

TOM

It's turned into some kind of funny picnic or something
which I don't like. I prefer to do it alone if I have to.

ED

We won't pay attention. We'll talk to each other.

DONNA

Right. (DONNA *crosses over to* ED *and* MOM *and sits on*

the floor; they gather around in a circle and talk, ignoring TOM.) Ed suggested we go up to his cabin, Mom, for the weekend.

ED
That's right.

MOM
Oh that'd be very fine. I'd like it. I certainly would. (TOM *turns back to the bookcase and starts hammering loudly again; the other three yell at each other.*)

DONNA
Such peace in the mountains!

MOM
Yes! And birds!

ED
Singing all the time!

DONNA
Such fun!

MOM
Lovely! Lovely! (TOM *throws down the hammer and goes out the door, slamming it behind him; the three stare at the door, then* DONNA *stands and picks up the hammer, she climbs slowly up on the stool with her back to the audience;* ED *and* MOM *watch her.*)

DONNA
The time I spent deciding which books to choose and how and why. All that time perusing tiny bookstore shelves and never a thought as to where they'd wind up. Never one little thought about how to store books, how to keep them.

ED
I know.

DONNA

And it could be so lovely, too. So very pleasing to the eyeball. With various sizes and shapes and groups together. Without concern for what they're about or what they mean to me and who wrote them when. Just in terms of size and shape and color.

MOM

Yes, dear.

DONNA

But I'm at a loss. I'm really not ready to hammer and nail just yet. I can't bring myself around to it. I'd like it all done. I'd like to see it all finished and done and through with. (ED *stands*.)

ED

I was going to— (DONNA *turns abruptly on the stool toward* ED.)

DONNA

Sit down!

ED

I started—

DONNA

Sit back down! (ED *sits on the lumber again*.) Do you have to feel guilty about something you have nothing to do with!

MOM

That's true.

DONNA

Do you! I didn't ask you to apologize to me for not having finished my bookcase. Did I! No I didn't. As a matter of fact I was talking to myself rather than to anyone in particular. I wasn't even conversing actually. Of course there was no way of your knowing that.

ED

I was just saying—

DONNA

You were just going to say that you felt bad inside your heart because you didn't finish my bookcase when you were supposed to. That instead of finishing you pawned the job off on my husband and went off on a nifty little vacation in the woods somewhere. And finally that you allowed my poor old mother to haul books up eight flights of stairs in the midst of her old age.

ED

I— (*The lights change to white; the door opens slowly and* POP *enters with his arms full of books, he crosses slowly down left and stacks the books in a pile, then sits on them with his back to the audience as the others watch.*)

MOM

There he is. I love him.

DONNA

But you don't need to. (*She turns slowly upstage again, facing the bookcase.*) It's quite all right with me. In fact it's perfect. It gives you something to project into the future as a future reference. Next time we'll know what to do. We'll have gathered together our joint experience and be able to use it as a kind of guidepost or maybe even a kind of guiding light.

POP

Boy, oh boy. Lots of stairs. I'll say that.

DONNA

(*Without turning around*) Lots of books, Pop. I'm glad to see you helping, even though it must be painful.

73

POP

There's many more. Never seen so many. Tons and tons down there. All piled up.

MOM

(*Still sitting stage right*) Poor baby. (ED *stands again.*)

ED

I should go down maybe. (DONNA *turns on the stool.*)

DONNA

No! Sit down there and stay sitting! (ED *sits back down.*) The books will make their way up gradually. Ever so slowly. They'll come up an arm load at a time. Carried by friends or relatives or people who might pass them accidentally and offer a helping hand.

ED

I'd like to help.

MOM

Yes, dear.

DONNA

That's fine. That's really all right but I've just decided against it, Ed. I've decided you might just gum up the works. And we can't have that. Not at this stage of the game.

POP

It's like climbing hills.

DONNA

Not that we have to be overly careful. But selectivity has its good points now and then.

POP

There's nothing like a climb now and then.

DONNA

After a while, in fact, you forget the whole business.

74

The preparation, the blueprint, the ideas, the measurements. We just pass through the room and take the whole shmear for granted.

MOM
Yes.

ED
I know, but I made it to order. It's precisely done. Just nail up the shelves and it could be considered a finished piece of work. Not even painted it would serve its purpose.

POP
What I was thinking was about a pulley. A dolly arrangement with heavy cables to pull up so many books as that.

MOM
Yes, dear.

DONNA
You mean out the window? Very good, Pop! Hang some pulleys out the window. (ED *stands.*) Where are you going now?

ED
My cabin.

MOM
Oh.

DONNA
That's right. A one-room place, right? In the woods somewhere?

ED
Yes.

DONNA
How did you come by such a nice little place as that?

ED

It was given—donated, rather.

MOM

Oh yes.

DONNA

It could be fixed into a year-round home, I imagine.

ED

That's what I'm working on.

DONNA

With heat and gas and electric lights all around. Like a Christmas house.

ED

Christmas?

POP

In the snow.

DONNA

Comfortable and homey, I imagine. Somehow I see it lost in the woods and nobody even living there.

ED

Really?

DONNA

Yes. And somehow it maintains itself all year round. Somehow it adapts itself to every change in the weather and turns on its own lights at night and then turns them off again in the morning. It even flushes its own toilet and builds its own fires and makes its little bed. There's no footprints around it at all. Just buried one quarter of the way in snow, and smoke coming out its chimney. Just sitting there in a small clearing about half a mile from a frozen lake. A Christmas house.

ED
There's no lake at all and I haven't even built the chimney yet.

POP
Oh too bad.

DONNA
But you're going to?

ED
I might.

DONNA
Well how will you stay there all year round if you don't have a chimney?

ED
Who says I'm staying?

DONNA
You did. You told me that.

ED
I might.

DONNA
You will. I can tell you will. You won't ever come back once you get all moved in.

ED
You make it sound very definite. Like I have no choice.

DONNA
I'm sorry.

ED
It's a place for retirement, if you really want to know. A place for resting and walking and not doing much else.

DONNA
Well that's fine then. You should have no trouble. This

then is your very last job on earth, I take it. And to think you're leaving it unfinished. That gets to me a little when I think of it. An unfinished piece of work.

ED

For Christ's sake, I finished the frame. (*The lights change to blue; the door opens and* TOM *enters, his arms full of books, he kicks the door shut, he stands holding the books and looking around at all the people.*)

TOM

You still here?

ED

I guess.

POP

Tommy boy.

TOM

Are you finishing up, my dear?

DONNA

Yes, I thought I would. (*She turns toward the bookcase and starts hammering loudly on the shelves; the rest yell their lines.*)

ED

I really have to leave! I'm sorry!

TOM

Well go then! Go! It's under control! It's not going to be hard at all, once we get it organized!

MOM

A Christmas house!

ED

But I'd like to help some more!

78

TOM

No need! We have enough hands as it is! You're only in the way! (DONNA *stops hammering but does not turn around,* TOM *still holds the books.*)

ED

I'm really sorry. Well all right. So long then. (ED *slowly crosses to the door and exits as the others watch him.*) 'Bye. (*He waves to them, then closes the door behind him.*)

DONNA

(*Still facing the bookcase*) Pop used to talk about a house like that when I was a girl and he was a father. How come you stopped thinking of that house, Pop? (TOM *crosses slowly to extreme stage right and sets the books in a pile, then sits on them with his back to the audience.*)

POP

Whereabouts?

MOM

Oh dear.

DONNA

How could it happen like that? I mean so easily. Without any regrets. To start hauling books for your very own daughter.

MOM

Yes, dear.

POP

They're all heavy.

DONNA

Not minding at all one way or the other. Letting things slip away from you as though it didn't matter. As though it were all a joke and talking about a Christmas house doesn't really mean there will ever be one. I can see that!

TOM

Donna! (*She turns slowly around on the stool and faces* TOM.)

DONNA

Yes, dear?

TOM

Shall we paint or not?

DONNA

Not just yet, I don't think. I don't care that much one way or the other.

TOM

We can't leave them plain. (*He crosses to the cans of paint and opens them.*)

DONNA

We could. Of course we could. If worse came to worse we could sit on the books all year round and forget about the shelves. Like a bunch of hens. How about it? They might even hatch.

MOM

Yes, dear. (TOM *kneels facing the audience and stirs the paint with one of the paintbrushes.*)

TOM

We can't leave it plain no matter how you look at it. We bought the paint already.

DONNA

That doesn't matter now. The color's unimportant. (*She gets down off the stool and crosses to the pile of books that* TOM *brought in, she picks a few of the books up; she turns as though to go back to the bookcase,* TOM *stands with the paintbrush in his hand.*)

TOM
Just leave the books where they are. (DONNA *stops and faces* TOM, *her arms full of books.*)

DONNA
Look. I don't give a damn any more about how it looks.

TOM
That's just too bad. We started it and now we'll finish.

DONNA
We started nothing. You never even wanted a bookcase at all. In the beginning.

TOM
But now it's there and it has to be finished.

DONNA
Has to be nothing. We leave it as it is. (*She approaches the bookcase.*)

TOM
Stay where you are! (DONNA *stops,* MOM *and* POP *remain indifferent throughout all this.*)

DONNA
Is it that important to you really? I mean in your heart of hearts?

TOM
Most important. It's become essential. It's become overpowering to me. Coloring every moment of my waking hours. I wake up thinking of this bookcase and I sleep dreaming of it. I walk around with the smell of it in my nose and I can see it in the future. I have a picture in my head of what it might become and I plan to fulfill that picture if it's the last thing I do.

DONNA
Swell! (*She drops the books abruptly on the floor,* TOM

*swings the paintbrush through the air so that paint
streaks down the front of Donna.) Shithead! (They stare
at each other but do not move,* MOM *and* POP *simultaneously pull a book out from each of their respective piles
and start reading them with their backs still to the audience.)*

TOM
I could have compromised a day or two ago while it was
still in the planning stage. But now it's too late. Now it's
definitely too late.

DONNA
You've become very definite very fast. *(She moves slowly
toward the second paintbrush as* TOM *stalks her, holding
the brush in front of him like a weapon.)*

TOM
I find it helps. I'm not so wishy-washy and I can make
fast decisions on a moment's notice.

DONNA
Right on top, as they say.

TOM
Exactly.

DONNA
Must be nice.

TOM
It is. I feel at home in any situation. I baffle everyone
around me and I'm known for my wit.

DONNA
A joy to be with.

TOM
Of course. *(*DONNA *grabs the other brush and dips it in
the paint,* TOM *makes a lunge toward her but backs away,*

they hold the brushes in front of them and crouch for attack.)

DONNA
People must flock to your side. You must have what they call "magnetism," a pulling sensation. That's the opposite of repulsion. Something like Yin and Yang.

TOM
Very close to it. *(They rush at each other and slap the brushes across each other's face—this should happen almost as though they were making a mockery of the fight, like two old gentlemen slapping each other with gloves—they back away and resume the crouch more typical of a street fight with knives.* MOM *and* POP *gradually turn toward the audience while sitting on their stacks of books, they become very engrossed in their reading,* POP *turns toward stage left and* MOM *toward stage right.)*

DONNA
How could it lie dormant for so many years? Just under the surface and itching to pop out.

TOM
I had no chance. No field to practice in. I'd throw rocks now and then but there was always something left over. Some extra zest.

DONNA
All the windows you broke in preparation. All the dirt clods you threw. And the people chasing you across acres of vacant lots, firing shotguns and swearing your name.

TOM
My name was death in the neighborhood. I hung around with enemies of the town. Even enemies of myself.

DONNA

But now! (*They charge and slap each other again with the brushes, then back away.*)

TOM

Yes! And my health has changed for the better. Even my eyes sparkle and my ears are clear. My whole body pulses with new life.

DONNA

The trouble is the longevity. Its lasting power. It seems like a stage to me. Just a frame of mind. Temporarily manic is the way I'd put it.

TOM

But that's so wrong. So easily overlooking what's right in front of you. You can't see the way my veins stand out? The way my temples throb? (*They charge and slap each other, this time more deliberately and enjoying it less, they back away.*)

DONNA

You'll fall back into it again. Wait and see. You'll sleep for days, afraid to get up. You'll wet your bed.

TOM

I'll jump out of bed! You don't even know. You haven't seen me when I'm at my best.

DONNA

You'll tremble under stacks of blankets, afraid to show your face. How will you account for the lies you've told?

TOM

Nothing false about it. I've gone through that stage. That pubic stage. (*By this time* MOM *and* POP *are directly facing the audience and remain that way to the end of the play, deeply absorbed in reading.*)

DONNA

Prone on your back forever and ever. You'll cry to be read to. You'll want a bedtime story twenty-four hours a day. And no lights. I'll have to read to you with a flashlight tucked under my arm. The room will be dark and you'll whimper until you fall asleep.

TOM

It could never happen now! (*They charge and viciously paint each other with the brushes, then back away; they are both covered with white paint by now.*)

DONNA

All you'll have is a tiny little glimmer of your present excitement. The rest will have gone and you'll lie there forever, trying to get it back. The bed will be your house and home and your head will be glued to the pillow. Your arms will be stuck to the sheet and your legs will be paralyzed from the hip down. You can't turn your head because you drool from the mouth and pus will run out your nose. Your eyes fill up with water and pour over onto your cheeks and each ear hums from hearing nothing. You lie in pools of urine and feces for days on end until the bed and you become one thing. One whole thing and there's no way of telling where the bed stops and you begin. You smell the same, you look the same, you act the same, you are the same. (*The lights change to white; the door opens and* ED *enters with his arms full of books, he kicks the door shut,* DONNA *and* TOM *drop the brushes on the floor and look at* ED, MOM *and* POP *keep reading.*)

ED

Hi.

DONNA AND TOM

Hi.

ED
Decided to bring up a load.

DONNA AND TOM
Good.

ED
Where should I set them?

DONNA AND TOM
Oh, anywhere is all right. (*Ed crosses and piles the books down center, then turns and looks at the bookcase.*)

ED
How's it coming?

DONNA AND TOM
Not bad.

ED
There's not as many down there as you had me believe. I mean by the way you were talking anybody would think you were flooded with books. But there's just a few. A couple more trips and you'll have it done.

DONNA AND TOM
We decided to stay.

ED
What? No, I mean a couple more trips up the stairs and you'd have it all finished. The books.

DONNA AND TOM
We're staying up here.

ED
Well I can't bring them all. One trip is all I have time for. It won't take very long and you forget the climb after a while. You were probably counting the flights as you came up. That's always bad. If you stop counting, it'll

go much faster. I can assure you of that. I personally find work to be easier if I distract myself rather than pour my full concentration into it. That way you forget about your body and therefore you're not conscious of being fatigued or exhausted. In fact I usually finish up a day's work fully refreshed. I know that seems odd to most people but it's true. Work tends to boost my energy rather than diminish it.

DONNA AND TOM
That does seem strange.

ED
The trouble is I don't have enough time. I wouldn't mind bringing the rest up for you but I really have to go.

DONNA AND TOM
That's quite all right. (*They both turn upstage and stare at the bookcase with their backs to* ED.)

ED
It's just too bad all the way around. We should all take some time off. You know? Why don't we do that? We could all go up there this very minute and take a little rest. We'd be just in time for the first snow. And we could make some kind of special dinner. You know, a turkey dinner with cranberry sauce. Then we could build a fire and sit around drinking hot chocolate. Then we could—

MOM AND POP
(*Reading from the books*) And the snow started early and came so soft that nobody even noticed. The only way they could really tell was the way the trees slowly changed from green to white.

ED
We could do that. It would just be a visit. I'm all moved in so I don't need any help.

MOM AND POP

It fell for hours and hours, then days and days, and it looked like it wouldn't stop. In fact everyone decided that it wouldn't stop and it kept going on. Falling down and down.

ED

There's really enough room even though it's small.

MOM AND POP

But the funny thing was that there wasn't any wind and there wasn't any cold. It just fell and changed everything from the color it was to white. But it got thicker and thicker so the people went outside but it didn't get any better. It got thicker and thicker and covered all their trees.

ED

I really can't hang around. I have to get back to my house now.

MOM AND POP

It got so bad that they had to climb a hill and watch from the top while their houses disappeared. It happened very slow but they never sat down and their legs got very strong.

ED

I'll even buy the food and cook it all myself.

MOM AND POP

It happened very slow and they stood very still until the smoke went away from their little chimney tops. Then the trees disappeared while they all just looked and didn't say a word but stood in a line looking straight ahead. The blanket moved up and the valley disappeared but the people didn't cry and it kept coming down and it kept piling up and they all just stared and didn't say a word.

ED

If I *could* stay I would! (*Everyone but* ED *says the next lines simultaneously in perfect synchronization.* MOM *and* POP *still reading and facing front,* DONNA *and* TOM *still facing the bookcase, and* ED *somewhere in the middle.*)

ALL BUT ED

The place was in white as far as they could see and not a sound or a wind or a hint of cold or hot. Not a taste in their mouth or a sting in their nose. And they moved very slow away from the place. And they moved and they moved and they didn't say a thing. Didn't laugh, didn't cry, didn't moan, didn't sigh, didn't even cough as the snow came down.

ED

It's just too bad!

ALL BUT ED

And once they turned they didn't turn around and once they walked they didn't even stop and they met more people as they went along, all new people as they went along, and the ground was white for as far as they could see and the sky was white, as white as it could be, and the crowd was thick and the air was thin but there wasn't any cold and there wasn't any hot and they couldn't even stop. (ED *joins in at this point as they all say the lines in perfect unison; they don't wait for* ED, *he simply joins them.*)

ALL

So they just moved on and on and on and as the story goes they never did stop, they never did drop, they never lagged behind or even speeded up. They never got tired and they never got strong and they didn't feel a thing. And nobody knows how they ever got lost, how they ever got away. To this very same day nobody knows how they ever got away. (*The lights change to blue, all the shelves fall off the bookcase onto the floor, none of the actors move; the blue light dims out very slowly to the end of the play,* MOM *and* POP *stand slowly as the other actors start to hum "White Christmas" very softly, begin picking up all the debris from the floor and carrying it off-stage through the door.* MOM *and* POP *read alternately from the book, staying on either side of the stage; the other three clean the entire stage, starting with the debris, then the books, then dismounting the entire set and taking it off so that the stage is completely bare by the end of the play; they hum the tune more loudly as they continue, likewise* MOM *and* POP *read more loudly.*)

POP

The original plan unfortunately hasn't changed, despite publicity to the contrary. The radial city exists much the same as it always has in the past. In fact it never really occurred out of a preconception on the part of individual architects or city planners.

MOM

It occurred more out of a state of frenzy and a complete lack of consideration for the future function of a place to live and/or work. The present condition is only the outcome of that lack of consideration.

POP

Consequently the city as it exists today affords certain people who live in certain areas many more benefits and varied ways of living than it does certain other people. This situation occurs in terms of center points similar to the hub of a wheel. The center of a city always offers people more diversions, more necessities, and more of everything they need to stay alive.

MOM

Therefore the center is densely populated and has a

90

greater coagulation of excitement in the air. The farther one gets from this center point the less one is aware of the excitement. As one moves toward the country and more rural areas the excitement has all but disappeared.

POP

The problem seems to be one of accommodating people with the pleasures and necessities of the city and at the same time offering them plenty of open green space— since city parks are nothing more than tiny breathing places or overly synthetic versions of the real thing and they also make it tremendously difficult to forget the city (if that be their function) for the simple fact that they were conceived in the midst of horrendous skyscrapers.

MOM

Skyscrapers, too, have never solved any congestive problems since they were built more out of the need for space than with any consideration for the human being. Hence when the day's work is done, there is a terrible conglomerate of people pushing their way out of the base of each building and rushing to more rural developments.

POP

The obvious alternative to this radial concept seems to be what might be called the "linear city" or the "universal city." As an example the city would stretch in a line from the tip of Maine to the tip of Florida and be no wider than a mile. The city would stop immediately at its mile width, at which point the country would commence. This would allow any citizen with the ability to use his or her legs to walk from the midst of the city into the midst of the country.

MOM

Unexcelled transportation systems would be put into use for the traversing of the city's length. An underground system traveling at the speed of two hundred miles an hour. An overhead system traveling at the rate of four hundred miles per hour. Two very wide belts, much like conveyor belts, would stretch from Florida to Maine and be in perpetual motion twenty-four hours a day, seven days a week. One belt moving at the rate of four miles per hour, the other at eight miles per hour.

POP

These would be primarily used for any person walking from someplace to someplace and if they couldn't afford the higher speed systems. A person walking on the four-mile-an-hour belt would obviously be walking four miles an hour faster than his normal pace. If he or she became tired he could then sit down on the eight-mile-an-hour belt and maintain the same speed.

MOM

Skyscrapers would be eliminated in preference to elongated parallel structures with many outlets along their sides. Thus eliminating heavy congestion at one exit.

POP

Cultural centers would be evenly distributed along the entire length of the city. Museums, concerts, movies, theater, etcetera would be readily available to everyone rather than the chosen few.

MOM

State borders would disintegrate and all police cars would be the same color as well as all license plates.

POP

Schools would be functional rather than regional and the children could walk to the country on their lunch hour.

MOM

Employment opportunities would vastly increase.

POP

Water shortage would be extinct.

MOM
Cross-country linear cities would develop.

POP
Stretching from coast to coast and crisscrossing the vertical cities.

MOM
The vertical cities stretching north through Canada and south through Mexico.

POP
All the way into South America.

MOM
Each city no less than ten miles from the next city.

POP
Forming ten-mile squares of country in between.

MOM
Desert cities and jungle cities where cities have never been.

POP
Ocean cities and sky cities and cities underground.

MOM
Joining country to country and hemisphere to hemisphere.

POP
Forming five-mile squares in between. (*The stage is bare by this time, the other three actors are off-stage but still humming the tune,* MOM *and* POP *still face front.*)

MOM
Elevated cities suspended under vacuum air.

POP
Forming two-mile squares in between.

MOM

Cities enclosed in glass to see the sky.

POP

Forming one-mile squares.

MOM

Cities in the sky to see the glass.

POP

Forming squares in between. (MOM *and* POP *close their books, the lights dim out, the other three actors stop humming off-stage.*)

The End

Red Cross

RED CROSS was first produced at the Judson Poets'
Theatre. It was directed by Jacques Levy and played by
Joyce Aaron, Lee Kissman, and Florence Tarlow.

NOTES ON *RED CROSS*

No curtain, all-white set and props—no other color visible—with white light full up all over the stage. When the audience enters, the intensity of what they see is blinding, like looking at snow in the sun. A new color is introduced —skin-color!—when the characters come on, but the costumes are white. During the longer middle section of the play, some lights dim slowly over a thirty-minute period, an imperceptible change—then, when Carol enters again, they bang up full. I am describing here some of the jolts that I chose to make the context for Sam's play as we did it at the Judson Poets' Theater. I tried to create a spare, clean, straight atmosphere, the air thin enough to transmit even small explosions a mile away. Startling things occurring in such a climate become magnified—the ending, followed by a sharp blackout, made a lot of people gasp, and there was always dead silence in the house until the lights came up for bows. To create such an atmosphere, the work of the actors must be sharp and crisp, and I worked toward getting them to slip in and out of character in ways designed to suddenly illuminate a particular facet of what was going on at the moment. And they didn't slowly glide in an out, but (snap!), did it like that—nothing hidden, everything in the clear. The actors were thereby able to abandon, at such times, what was "natural" or "organic" for the character and to show instead a strong image of what the character was doing. Examples: Carol's long "snow" speech at the beginning was done, for the most part, in the manner of an excited radio sportscaster, perched on her bed in a still-photo pose of a skier. Jim's "swimming lesson" was delivered like a drill sergeant's rendering of a military manual. And the Maid's "drowning" was partly gusto-laughter, partly crying, partly a put-on to show Jim (and the audience) where she was at—it was really funny to watch, until she ended with the speech about becoming a fish, and then it all switched suddenly and having exhausted Jim, there she was, on her knees facing the audience, taking time to brush her hair back from her face before speaking, all the wildness of a moment ago completely gone; and when she spoke, it was very directly to the audience, to individuals out there, the actress talking in her own natural voice, quietly and simply, not unlike a simple recitation to an interested group of friends. Not gimmicks, but a wish to follow to the limits the specific intention of a moment in the play, to highlight it, as bursting into color in the midst of a black-and-white film would do. If Jim, in his game-playing attempt to involve the Maid, proceeds into an overblown pseudo-soliloquy about his infirmity ("I climbed a tree one day . . ."), then why not push it that extra step and have him do it like a jaded, over-the-hill Shakespearean player. The actor thus makes visible that image which relates most closely to what the character is doing, irrespective of whether that character would "naturally" act in such a way. When the Maid spoke to the audience, it became visibly obvious that she had left Jim back in the quagmire of his own making, left him back at the launching pad. Having someone take you more seriously than you take yourself (as happened to Jim) is enough to make anybody's "head blow up," as one teenage member of the audience put it.

Red Cross is a cool play—in the sense that it is dense, not brought to the point of intellectual clarity, embedded in a series of metaphors which are all interconnected— and because it is a cool play, it must be treated as such, *not* "hotted up" by filling in the seemingly empty places where not enough is said to make for clear, unitary, conscious meaning. (Two facts are relevant here: [1] Sam can be extraordinarily precise and articulate whenever he feels the necessity of it; [2] He is not a willful obscurantist.) Sam is more interested in *doing* something to audiences than in saying something to them, and what he wants to do has no relationship to the purging of emotions through identification or total involvement. It is more like the way changing a room's temperature does something to the people in it. And because the writing is cool, one must continually skirt the big sucking vacuum-trap of trying to make those astounding verbal trips into some kind of imagist poetry (like Dylan Thomas reciting Bob Dylan). To be simultaneously involved and detached as the play is, as a surgical operation is, as a cat staring is—that's the trick for a production of this play. And I can give no good advice on how to do that, except to have Sam sitting back there during rehearsals, ready to give you the raspberry if you start to get a bit corny, even more ready to start chuckling and making funny faces and gassing himself when something that he's so far seen only in his head suddenly happens on the stage.

Jacques Levy

SCENE

The bedroom of a cabin. There is a screen door up center leading out to a small porch. A window stage left and stage right. There are twin beds, one under each window with the heads facing upstage. The tops of trees can be seen through the screen door and each of the windows to give the effect of a second story. As the lights come up JIM *is sitting on the bed to stage left facing* CAROL, *who is sitting on the other bed. Everything in the set plus costumes should be white.*

CAROL
Look at it closely.

JIM
I am.

CAROL
You can't see it, then?

JIM
Yes.

CAROL
Then it *is* bad. I can't believe it. The tingling. It's like a tingling thing under each eye. It goes into the nose, too.

JIM
Maybe it's just sinus or something.

CAROL
No. I can see the results. If you can see something happening, then it couldn't just be sinus. The whole face and ears and nose and eyes. And my hands. Feel my hands. (*She holds her hands out, Jim holds them.*)

JIM
Hm. (*She pulls her hands back.*)

CAROL

Feel them? What's that, Jim. Something's happening. My hands never sweat like that. And my feet. Hold my foot. (*She raises her foot,* JIM *holds it.*) Just feel it. The other one, too. Feel them both. What's that? Under the eyes is what bothers me. It's from wearing those glasses. I can tell. It's from the glasses. My head aches so bad. I can't believe my head.

JIM

Why?

CAROL

It hurts. It's breaking open all the time. It crashes around inside. (*She gets up and starts pacing around the stage as* JIM *remains sitting on the stage left bed.*)

JIM

What's the matter?

CAROL

It's anything. Beer or water or too many cigarettes and it starts to break. One day it'll break clear open and I'll die, I'll be dead then.

JIM

Take it easy.

CAROL

It'll just burst and there I'll be lying in the middle of the street or in a car or on a train. With a bursted head.

JIM

Somebody will take care of you.

CAROL

It might happen when I'm skiing or swimming.

JIM

There's always lots of people around those places. They'll see you and help.

CAROL

They'll see my head. (*She crosses to the stage right bed and stands on it facing* JIM *and begins to act out the rest as though she were skiing on a mountain slope.*) It'll be in the snow somewhere. Somewhere skiing on a big white hill. In the Rockies. I'll be at the top of this hill and everything will be all right. I'll be breathing deep. In and out. Big gusts of cold freezing air. My whole body will be warm and I won't even feel the cold at all. I'll be looking down and then I'll start to coast. Very slowly. I'm a good skier. I started when I was five. I'll be halfway down and then I'll put on some steam. A little steam at first and then all the way into the egg position. The Europeans use it for speed. I picked it up when I was ten. I'll start to accumulate more and more velocity. The snow will start to spray up around my ankles and across my face and hands. My fingers will get tighter around the grips and I'll start to feel a little pull in each of my calves. Right along the tendon and in front, too. Everything will be working at once. All my balance and strength and breath. The whole works in one bunch. There'll be pine trees going past me and other skiers going up the hill. They'll stop and watch me go past. I'll be going so fast everyone will stop and look. They'll wonder if I'll make it. I'll do some jumps and twist my body with the speed. They'll see my body twist, and my hair, and my eyes will water from the wind hitting them. My cheeks will start to sting and get all red. I'll get further and further into the egg position with my arms tucked up. I'll look down and see the valley and the cars and houses and people walking up and down. I'll see all the cabins with smoke coming out the chimneys. Then it'll come. It'll start like a twitch in my left ear. Then I'll start to feel a throb in the bridge of my nose. Then a thump in the base of my neck. Then a crash right through my skull. Then I'll be down. Rolling! Yelling! All those people will see it. I'll be rolling with my skis locked and my knees buckled under me and my arms thrashing through the snow. The skis will cut into both my legs and I'll bleed all over. Big gushes of red all over the snow. My arms will be broken and dragging through the blood. I'll smell cocoa and toast and marmalade coming out of the cabins. I'll hear dogs barking and see people pointing at me. I'll see the road and college kids wearing sweat shirts and ski boots. Then my head will blow up. The top will come right off. My hair will blow down the hill full of guts and blood. Some bluejay will try to eat it probably. My nose will come off and my whole face will peel away. Then it will snap. My whole head will snap off and roll down the hill and become a huge snowball and roll into the city and kill a million people. My body will stop at the bottom of the hill with just a bloody stump for a neck and both arms broken and both legs. Then there'll be a long cold wind. A whistle, sort of. It'll start to snow a little bit. A very soft easy snow. The squirrels might come down to see what happened. It'll keep snowing very lightly like that for a long time until my whole body is covered over. All you'll see is this little red splotch of blood and a whole blanket of white snow.

VOICE OFFSTAGE
Miss Littles! Miss Littles, are you ready!

CAROL
What?

JIM
You have to go.

102

CAROL

Oh. Yes. (*She crosses to the door, she opens the door and yells down.*) I'll be right there! (*She crosses to* JIM *and kisses him on the forehead.*) You'll meet me, right? Please?

JIM

Yes.

CAROL

I'll see you then at six. (*She kisses him again.*) Six o'clock.

JIM

Right. (*She exits.* JIM *gets up and crosses to the door, he hums some kind of tune, he looks out, then goes back to the bed and sits, he scratches his legs, then he stands up and takes his pants off, he sits back down and starts scratching his legs, he starts picking little bugs out of his skin and then stepping on them, he gets up and starts doing pushups downstage center. A* MAID *appears on the porch through the screen door, holding two pillows, sheets, and bedspreads in her arms, she is rather fat and older than* JIM, *she watches* JIM *as he does his pushups, then she knocks on the door;* JIM *continues, she knocks again, then a third time very loudly.*)

JIM

(*Still doing pushups*) Come in, come in, come in. Have a seat or something.

MAID

It's the maid, dear.

MAID

(*Without turning to look*) Come in, come in and have a bed or a seat. Whatever you want.

MAID

(*Still on the porch*) I want to change the beds is all.

MAID

(*He stops and turns to her, sitting on the floor.*) Well come in. The beds are in here.

MAID

Thank you. (*She enters and sets the linen down on the stage right bed,* JIM *sits on the floor looking at her.*) I always seem to catch you, don't I?

JIM

Yep. You catch me every time. I think you plan it.

MAID

No.

JIM

I think you do. You like catching me.

MAID

It's just the time of day. You're the only one left this time of day.

JIM

Come on. Where do they go?

MAID

It's true.

JIM

Where do they go? I've seen them around during the day. They hang around. They play tennis or something.

MAID

I just make the beds.

JIM

You know where they go. They go into town. Right?

104

(*She starts to change the stage left bed.*) Hey leave my bed alone! (*He stands.*)

MAID
Well I have to change it, dear.

JIM
It's got stains. I don't want you to see the stains. I get embarrassed. (*He jumps on the stage left bed facing the* MAID.) I do. It embarrasses me. I get pink and everything.

MAID
All right. (*She turns and starts making the other bed.*) I've seen yellow spots before, you know. It don't bother me.

JIM
Well it bothers me. I get pink.

MAID
I'm sorry about that.

JIM
Do you know anything about crabs?

MAID
About what?

JIM
Crabs. Bugs that get in your pubic hair and eat your skin and suck your blood and make you itch.

MAID
Like nits or something?

JIM
What's a nit?

MAID
Like lice.

JIM

Yeah. Except on a smaller scale. Almost microscopic. With legs and red heads. They twitch when you grab hold of them. I can show you one if you want to see it. Do you want to see one?

MAID

Not really.

JIM

Oh, come on.

MAID

All right. (*Jim sits on the edge of the bed and picks at his legs, the* MAID *sits on the other bed facing him, he gets hold of a small bug and hands it carefully to the* MAID, *who looks at it in the palm of her hand.*) They must be part of the lice family to get in your skin.

JIM

There. See it? They crawl around.

MAID

Mm. You got these all over?

JIM

No. They're localized.

MAID

Can't you get some medicine? (*She hands the bug back to Jim.*)

JIM

I don't want it back.

MAID

Well I don't want it.

JIM

Throw it on the floor. (*She throws it down,* JIM *steps on it.*) What kind of medicine?

MAID

Sheep dip or something.

JIM

Sheep dip! (*He stands on the bed again.*) Why sheep dip?

MAID

I'm sorry. (*She starts changing the bed again.*)

JIM

Sheep dip is for woolly animals or dogs or something. Human lice are different from animal lice. The whole treatment is different.

MAID

Well that's the only thing I can tell you.

JIM

Who uses sheep dip for crabs? That's ridiculous. I mean that's really stupid.

MAID

Well I don't know, then. You'll have to find something pretty soon, though.

JIM

Why?

MAID

Well if I had parasites eating off me and draining me of all my blood and reducing my physical strength twenty-four hours a day, making me weaker and weaker while they got stronger and stronger, I can tell you that I'd do something. I'd get it taken care of. That's all I know. And I'm not smart.

JIM

You'd put sheep dip on them and kill your skin along with the crabs. Is that it?

107

MAID

I'd have enough sense to have my bed changed, knowing that crabs lay eggs inside the sheets and the blankets and that eggs hatch and that when eggs hatch new crabs are born. Baby crabs are born and baby crabs grow up like all crabs have to. And when they're grown they lay new crabs and it goes on and on like that indefinitely for years.

JIM

I'm talking about the immediate possibilities of killing the live crabs that are already there. Not the ones that haven't been born, maidy, maidy.

MAID

How 'bout a doctor?

JIM

Terrific. (*He jumps off the bed and crosses down center, doing arm exercises.*) I'm in the middle of the forest and you're talking about a doctor. Thank you. A country doctor, I suppose.

MAID

Isn't there someone to take you?

JIM

Not till six.

MAID

Can you wait?

JIM

I don't know. They really get to me every once in a while. You know what I mean? They pinch so hard I think they're going all the way through. They grab and squeeze. I think they must have teeth too. Along with the pincers I think they have teeth.

MAID

Can you wait till six?

JIM

(*He crosses right.*) It's a long time to go on itching like this. To have any itchy skin, I mean. And they're moving up, too. They've gotten to my navel and yesterday I found one in my armpit. Six is a long way off when this is happening to me. (*He crosses left.*) I can ignore them for periods of time. An hour at the longest if I'm preoccupied with something else. If I concentrate. They go away and then come back. It depends on the concentration. (*He stops doing the arm exercise.*)

MAID

I could take you. I have a car.

JIM

I climbed a tree yesterday and it went away for a couple hours. I climbed all over the tree. Through the branches and clear up to the top. I sat up there for a couple hours smoking cigarettes. That did it for a while. Then I went swimming and that helped. Swimming always helps. Then I ran around the lake at a medium fast trot. I jogged all the way around. I got up a good sweat and I was breathing very hard and my heart was pounding. All the blood was going through me at once.

MAID

Have you had them for a long time?

JIM

I've had crabs for about ten years now and it gets worse every year. They breed very fast. It's nice, though. It's like having two bodies to feed.

MAID

Well I could take you. I have a car. (JIM *turns to her.*) Do you want to go now?

JIM

You drive in every day?

MAID

Well I don't walk.

JIM

You drive from town all the way into the middle of the forest to change somebody else's beds?

MAID

That's right.

JIM

Aren't there any beds in town?

MAID

I like the drive.

JIM

Me too. It's nice. Calm. Smooth. Relaxing. Comfortable. Leisurely. Pleasurable. Enchanting. Delightful.

MAID

Yes.

JIM

Is there a doctor in town, did you say?

MAID

Well sure. I suppose. We could probably find one if you want to go.

JIM

There isn't one out here, huh? I mean they don't by any chance have a country doctor out in this neck of the woods. One a' them country guys in a model T Ford and a beat-up leather bag full of sheep dip. Maybe even a veterinarian. I hear veterinarians can take as good care of you as a physician or a real doctor. Have you heard that?

MAID

Do you want to go into town or not?

JIM
Gee! I'd like the ride. I'd like that a lot. To ride in the
car into town and get this taken care of. And then ride
back. That'd be a lot of trips for you to take, though. A
lot of extra hauls. Out and back and out and back. Coming and going.

MAID
I don't mind.

JIM
I could give you some gas money.

MAID
Forget it.

JIM
I insist. I absolutely insist.

MAID
Look—

JIM
Hey! Hold it! Hold it! I have an idea.

MAID
What?

JIM
You'll have to help me. Are you willing to help me?

MAID
I guess.

JIM
Okay. Come on. (*He starts pulling the stage right bed
down center.*) Push. Push it. (*The* MAID *starts pushing
the head of the bed as* JIM *pulls.*) Come on, push. Push.
Hup, hup.

111

MAID

What's this for?

JIM

You'll see. Come on. Get it down here. Hup, hup. Heave ho!

MAID

I have to go pretty soon, you know.

JIM

It won't take long. (*They pull the bed downstage, then* JIM *crosses to the stage left bed.*) Very good. Beautiful. Come on now. Help me with this. Come on. Hup, hup.

MAID

All right. (*They push the stage left bed across stage into the former position of the other bed.*) What are you doing?

JIM

Rearranging. It'll be much nicer. Much, much nicer. More better for everyone concerned. Hup, two. Hup, two.

MAID

I don't know.

JIM

Heave ho! (*They get the bed into position, then* JIM *crosses down to the other bed.*) All right, maidy baby. The last lap. Come on. It's almost done. Have faith. (*The* MAID *crosses down to the bed and helps him push it stage left.*) Heave, heave. Push, push. Put your back into it! A little more sweat there. Hup, two. 'At's it! Beautiful! Muy bien! Que bonita! (*He jumps on top of the stage left bed, the* MAID *sits on the stage right bed facing him.*) Esta es demasiado! (*He jumps up and down on the bed.*) Que bella! Que bella! Muy bien!

112

MAID
Why did you do that?

JIM
(*He stops jumping.*) Now I have a clean bed, right? A changed bed. New, fresh, white, clean sheets imported from town. A downy, soft, airy pillow and a freshly washed bedspread. Guaranteed to be free of crabs and crab eggs and lice and ticks and nits. Guaranteed to smell sweet and pure. I have all this and you didn't even have to change my old bed. Isn't that nice? Now we don't have to go to town at all. We can stay here and jump around.

MAID
Yes. (*She gets up and starts changing the stage right bed.*) And I'm all worn out.

JIM
Now what are you doing! Leave that bed alone! Stop that!

MAID
It's no longer yours, remember? We just switched. The one you're standing on is yours. You can't have both, you know. Make up your mind.

JIM
It doesn't matter. Leave it alone! You'll catch something!

MAID
You're getting very selfish, aren't you? You forget somebody else sleeps in this bed. Somebody else who might not like to catch crabs.

JIM
She doesn't care! (*He flops down on the bed and lies on his stomach with his head toward the audience as the* MAID *continues to change the stage right bed.*)

MAID
I know she doesn't.

JIM
Is this the last room you have?

MAID
Yep.

JIM
You save it for last?

MAID
No. I just make a point to come here last. I keep hoping one day I'll come and you won't be here. All I'll have to do is come into this room and make the beds and go right back out. One day I'll be able to do this room in no time at all and just go straight home. What a day that will be.

JIM
You go straight home from here?

MAID
That's right.

JIM
You don't hang around at all?

MAID
Nope.

JIM
You don't hang around to climb a tree or run around the lake or nothing? You should come at night, maidy. You'd like it better at night. We could go swimming.

MAID
No thanks.

JIM
It's really better at night. You'd be surprised the way it

changes. All the different sounds and the air gets wetter. Sometimes it rains. That's the best time for swimming. When it rains. That way you get completely wet. A constant wetness.

MAID
Don't you catch cold?

JIM
No. Not a chance. Your body stays warm inside. It's just the outside that gets wet. It's really neat. I mean you can dive under water and hold your breath. You stay under for about five minutes. You stay down there and there's nothing but water all around you. Nothing but marine life. You stay down as long as you can until your lungs start to ache. They feel like they're going to burst open. Then just at the point where you can't stand it any more you force yourself to the top. You explode out of the water, gasping for air, and all this rain hits you in the face. You ought to try it.

MAID
I'm too fat for swimming.

JIM
What do you mean? You won't sink. You just do the strokes, you know. (*He starts kicking his feet and stroking with his arms.*) You learn how to breathe and you kick and you stroke and there's nothing to it. (*The MAID turns and looks at him.*) You know how, don't you?

MAID
Not really. I can never put it all together. I mean I either stroke faster than I kick or vica versa.

JIM
Watch me. It's easy once you get started. (*He starts going through the motions as the MAID watches.*) The kick-

ing is important. You have to keep your legs straight and kick from the waist. No bending the knees. And the arms too. Once the arm hits the water on the downsweep, you have to keep it straight. No bending from the elbow.

MAID
(She tries to copy him, moving her arms in an arc.) Do you keep your elbow straight?

JIM
Well no. Just as it goes through the water. That's the only time you have to worry. You can bend it as you take it back. Lie down over there and watch me. *(She lies down on the stage right bed with her head toward the audience, she watches JIM as he demonstrates the Australian crawl.)* Now the coordination has to come from knowing how to synchronize the speed. The rate of speed that your feet are taking has to match that of your stroking speed. The reason you can't put the two together is because you're not concentrating on the whole mechanism. That is, you're becoming more concerned with one end or the other rather than the collaboration of the two as a total unit.

MAID
I see.

JIM
Now start out slowly, keeping that in mind. *(She starts doing the crawl, JIM watches her for a while, then starts doing it himself.)* Keep it slow, trying to work on the points where you derive the most power. Think of the way an oar or a paddle is constructed. Regard your arms and legs as being paddles. A paddle has a broad surface and reaches its highest point of thrust when it is perpendicular to the surface line of the water. This is the way you should use your arms. Keep your fingers close

together to make a broader surface. Be careful not to let any water pass between them. That's it. Now the breathing is important. This requires added concentration and coordination. You will be able to breathe instinctively in the right manner if you keep in mind that the human being cannot inhale water.

MAID
(*Still doing the stroke*) Really?

JIM
Your head should pivot on your shoulders, always to the left. Inhale as your head comes out of the water and exhale as it goes into the water. Breathe in. Breathe out. In, out. In, out. (*They both breathe and continue the stroking.*)

MAID
In, out. In, out.

JIM
One, two. One, two. That's right. Remember the whole thing is working at once.

MAID
I'm getting tired.

JIM
It's no sweat. Keep it up. You can't poop out in the middle of a lake. Stroke! Stroke! Keep it moving. One, two. One, two. Atta girl.

MAID
It's my back. There's a pain in my back. (*She continues to swim,* JIM *goes faster.*)

JIM
That's good. It's good when it hurts. It's working then. Keep it up! We've almost got it. Hup, two! Hup, two!

MAID

It really aches, Jim.

JIM

That's all right. We're halfway already.

MAID

I'll never make it! My back.

JIM

Use it all. Everything at once. Make it work. One, two. One, two. (*He is going very fast with perfect coordination.*) In, out. In, out. Breathe! Breathe!

MAID

My leg! I've got a cramp, Jim! (*She continues very slowly.*)

JIM

Hup, two! Hup, two! Shake it off. Use it! Keep using it so it doesn't tighten. Keep it loose! Hup, two! Hup, two!

MAID

My side now! It's in my side!

JIM

Move it! Work it out! Keep it up!

MAID

Oh my leg! I can't. I can't do it! (*She continues slowly.*) It's killing me!

JIM

We're almost there! (*The* MAID *screams in agony, she lies very still on the bed with her face in the blanket,* JIM *stops and looks at her, he sits on the edge of the bed.*) Did you drown, maidy? (*She remains very still.*) Did maidy drown in the middle of the lake? Tsk, tsk, tsk, tsk.

MAID

I got a cramp.

JIM
A leg cramp and a side cramp. What a shame.

MAID
It's not very funny.

JIM
I guess we can't go then, right?

MAID
Go where?

JIM
Swimming. At night. Night swimming. Swimming in
the dark in the middle of the forest. Like we wanted to
do. Remember?

MAID
We could if you'd take it slower. If you wouldn't rush.
How can I learn all that in one sitting? In, out. In, out.
Breathe! Breathe! You can make it! I'm not an advanced
swimmer, you know. I'm not even an intermediate swimmer. I'm a beginner. I know nothing about swimming
and suddenly I'm supposed to have everything under my
belt. Just intuitively I'm supposed to. It's pretty unfair,
Jim.

JIM
I know.

MAID
If I get a cramp, I get a cramp. I can't go plodding on
like an Olympic champion or something. Jesus Christ.

JIM
I'm sorry.

MAID
It takes time to be a swimmer. (*She sits up on the bed,*
JIM *remains where he is.*) I can't just become a swimmer

119

in one lesson like that. I mean what is that? There's no
water or anything and you expect me to swim! How can
I swim on a bed! How can I do it!

JIM
I don't know.

MAID
I don't know either. I really don't. I can see me in a lake.
Can you imagine me in a lake in the middle of the night
with nobody around? Me and you in the middle of the
forest, in the middle of a lake. And there you are, fifty
yards ahead of me yelling: "In, out! In, out! You can
make it! You can make it! Keep it up!" (*She stands and
crosses down center, limping and holding her side.*) And
I'm sinking fifty yards behind you. That's what I'd be
doing, you know. Do you know that! I'd be sinking!

JIM
Yes.

MAID
Yes. The maid is slowly sinking. Gurgling, yelling, floundering for help. Sinking to the bottom of the lake on
her first swimming lesson. Her first time out.

JIM
Well take it easy. It's not my fault. (*The* MAID *limps more
deliberately and holds her side in mock agony.*)

MAID
The maid bobbing up and down, up and down with her
hands slapping the water, her mouth gasping for air, her
side screaming with pain.

JIM
I thought you'd swam before.

MAID
Wading is what I did before! Tiptoeing in shallow water

with my sneakers on! Not in seventy-five feet of lake water with no one around. Stranded there at night with my family in town and me in the forest and you wandering around smoking cigarettes in a tree and not giving a damn at all! (JIM *stands and crosses to the* MAID.)

JIM
Try to keep it moving. Work it out.

MAID
I can't now. It's cramped for good. I'll never swim again.

JIM
I know but keep it going. Keep the blood moving.

MAID
It'll never work. The pain is unbelievable.

JIM
Come on. Hup, two! Hup, two! You can make it.

MAID
Nobody able to eat at home because I'm drowning out here! Nobody knowing where I am. Everybody forgetting my name! And I'm getting worse all the time! I'm sinking more and more! With seaweed up my nose and tangled all around me and I can't see a thing in the night! (*She sinks to her knees and starts crawling around the stage on all fours as* JIM *follows her.*)

JIM
Will you please cut it out?

MAID
So you don't like me screaming out here, is that it? You don't like me getting carried away with my cramps and my pain in the middle of the night, in the middle of the forest. Well let me tell you it hurts me to do it. I don't like screaming myself. I try to keep a calm house, an

easy home with everyone quiet and happy. It's not an easy thing, Jim. At my age, in my condition.

JIM
Get up off the floor.

MAID
I make the beds and cook the meals. Everyone gets fed on time at my house.

JIM
I don't care. It's six o'clock now!

MAID
So the screaming shouldn't hurt you at all, knowing I don't do it all the time. Knowing that I save it for special times when my side starts to ache and my legs collapse and the water gets into my nose.

JIM
We can get you a doctor but you have to get up. (*She collapses on the floor and stays very still with* JIM *standing over her.*) Come on. I'll take you into town.

MAID
But once it's over it isn't bad at all. Once you get over the shock of having water all around and dragonflies and water lilies floating by and little silver fish flashing around you. Once that's past and you get all used to your flippers and your fins and your new skin, then it comes very easy. (*She stands slowly with no concern at all for her cramps and gathers together all the dirty laundry as she continues to talk.*) You move through the water like you were born in that very same place and never even knew what land was like. You dive and float and sometimes rest on the bank and maybe chew on some watercress. And the family in town forgets where you went and the swimming coach forgets who you are and *you* forget

all about swimming lessons and just swim without knowing how and before you know it the winter has come and the lake has frozen and you sit on the bank staring at the ice. You don't move at all. You just sit very still staring at the ice until you don't feel a thing. Until your flippers freeze to the ground and your tail freezes to the grass and you stay like that for a very long time until summer comes around. (*She glances at* JIM *and then exits out the door with the linen;* JIM *stares after her for a second, then rushes toward the door.*)

JIM

Hey! I could drive you home! (*He opens the door and looks out.*) Hey! Do you want a lift! (*He shuts the door, then turns downstage; he pauses, then rushes to his pants, he starts to put his pants on hurriedly, he gets them halfway on and* CAROL *enters, she is carrying a bag of groceries and wearing glasses, the door slams behind her,* JIM *looks at her for a second, then finishes putting on his pants,* CAROL *sets the groceries down on the stage left bed.*)

CAROL

Well. Guess what. A funny little thing. A very funny thing. I'm in the grocery store, see. I'm standing there looking for bread or something and guess what?

JIM

What?

CAROL

I start itching. (*She crosses down right;* JIM *stands center with his back to the audience, staring at the door.*) Not just a simple itch but a burn. A searing kind of thing. A biting, scratching thing that's tearing at me, see. (JIM *crosses slowly upstage and stands looking out the screen door.*) Well I'm paralyzed. I don't know what to do because it's all up my legs and under my arms. (*She walks back and forth downstage.*) I can't start scratching my private zones right in the middle of a grocery store. So I run to the bathroom. I make a beeline for the bathroom and I lock the door and I rip my clothes off. I literally tear them off my body. And I look. And do you know what it is? Bugs! Bugs all over me. Buried in my skin. Little tiny itty bitty bugs, clawing and biting at me. They're all in my hair and everything. Sucking my blood, Jim! They're actually in my skin. I've been carrying them around with me. And do you know what? I have a sneaking suspicion that they're in this room. I picked them up from being in this room. I'll bet they're right inside here. In the beds even. (*She goes to the stage right bed and rips off the bedspread and sheets.*) They're breeding in these beds. I'll bet you any amount of money. These cabins are so old and filthy. I bet they've been here for years without anybody checking. Bedbugs are no joke, Jim. I mean they suck your blood and everything. (*She goes to the other bed and tears it apart.*) I can't stand it. Just thinking about it upsets me. We'll have to get another room. That's all there is to it. Either that or go back home. I really can't take it. It's awful. Jim! (JIM *turns to her slowly, there is a stream of blood running down his forehead.*)

JIM
What?

CAROL
What happened!

JIM
When? (*BLACKOUT*)

The End

Melodrama Play

A MELODRAMA WITH MUSIC

NOTES ON *MELODRAMA PLAY*

Melodrama Play is unproduced.* A production of this play should not be aimed toward making it strictly satirical but more toward discovering how it changes from the mechanism of melodrama to something more sincere. This change does not just occur slowly from one thing into the other in the course of the play but rapidly as well and very frequently, especially in the case of Dana. There are no stage directions indicating when these changes should take place because some of them appear obvious to me and many of them do not. So I would rather leave their selection up to a director in any case. The selections themselves can also range from the most elaborate down to the most subtle. The band should behave like an additional audience, with dictated reactions to the play instead of spontaneous ones. When they sing, it should be as though they were performing in a discothèque and likewise when the actors dance. This also should be the case when Cisco sings his song but not necessarily when Duke sings. It might be helpful if a musician were cast as Cisco instead of an actor. It seems to me that everything about the play should be abrupt and flashy, except toward the end when Peter gets into his history. It might also be nice to have the band suspended from the ceiling in a cage over the audience's head.

Sam Shepard

*Editor's note: Since the above was written *Melodrama Play* has been produced by the La Mama Repertory. The original score was composed by Tom O'Horgan. Mr. O'Horgan also directed the production.

SCENE

*(A room. In the center of the upstage wall is a door.
Stage right of the door on the wall is a huge black and
white photograph of Bob Dylan without eyes. Stage left
of the door is an equally large photo of Robert Goulet
without eyes. A sofa against the stage left wall. A small
table at the downstage end of the sofa with a radio on it.
A piano against the stage right wall. An electric guitar
lies on the floor down center with a speaker and ampli-
fier facing the audience. There is a four-piece rock-and-
roll band seated in a cage on top of a platform at the back
of the audience all dressed exactly like* DUKE. *They stand
to sing their songs, then sit back down when they're finished. The lights come up fast.* DUKE DURGENS *enters very
fast through the door wearing extra long hair, shades,
jeans, boots, vest, etc. He crosses directly downstage
center, bows to the audience, and begins to improvise the
following song without accompaniment.)*

DUKE
Everybody knows that everybody grows
And everybody starts out fast
And everybody knows that anybody knows
How to make it last and last
And everybody says that you shouldn't snoop around
You shouldn't put your nose down to the ground
You shouldn't say out loud what we already know
You should say it to yourself
You should play it by yourself
You should keep it in your mouth
You should hold it in your throat
Even if you bloat
Even if you get to the point where you burst.

*(He stomps his foot on the ground and stops the song;
he paces up and down, mumbling to himself and hitting*

his fist into his hand; he does this for a while, then stops and bows again to the audience. DANA, *a girl with long hair, boots, jeans, leather jacket, shades, etc., enters fast with an envelope in her hand and sits on the sofa, she opens the envelope and pulls out a letter which she reads to herself while* DUKE *starts singing again to the audience.*)

DUKE
Nobody knows where the pain got started
It's still the same as it always was
Nobody sees how the pain gets started
So it just goes on like it always does
But if you'll come around to the back of my shack
If you'll come around when your legs start sagging
Then I know a way to stop you from gagging
I know a way to rest your head
But if you go on like you always do
If you go on thinking you're so true
Then the day will come when we'll all be dead
Without ever knowing what we could have done instead
So if you'll come around to the back of my shack . . .

(*He stomps his foot again and paces up and down as before.*)

DANA
How's it going?

DUKE
You heard. Shit. Garbage. Stuff I could have done in school behind everyone's back. Boy. It's terrible. Just terrible. I don't know what to do.

DANA
You got a letter.

DUKE
Good. (*Continuing to pace*)

DANA
I'll read it out loud.

DUKE
Thank you.

DANA
(*Reading the letter*) "Dear Mr. Durgens: I am a sociologist at Corning University and am currently engaged in a study of contemporary American musicians. I would like to ask you to participate in this study. My main interest is in discovering what changes occur in the life of a singer when one of his songs is received and acclaimed by the public at large. For example, how did you go about getting your first song, 'Prisoners, Get up out of Your Homemade Beds,' recorded and once it became a hit how did this affect your life?" (DUKE *starts singing as he continues to pace,* DANA *stops reading.*)

DUKE
Won't you pretty please move a little to the left
Won't you pretty please move a little to the right
Won't you shake your ass
Won't you shake your tits
Won't you please shake, baby, before I have fits
Wow!

DANA
Could I continue, please.

DUKE
Please do! Please continue on. There's more coming and if that's true I certainly would not want to be the one to block it from coming. Not me! Not I! After all, who am I to say stop! Stop coming, my dear? Not me.

DANA
Thanks. (*She continues with the letter as* DUKE *paces.*)

"After the public response to 'Prisoners, Get up out of Your Homemade Beds,' did your relations with friends, colleagues, and others in the music business change? Did you begin work on a new song or go back to work you had done previously? Did new opportunities become available in other media, etc.?"

DUKE

Yes! Oh yes. Mr.—Mr.—who?

DANA

Mr. Damon.

DUKE

Yes, Mr. Damon. Certainly. Vistas opened out and up and all around me. I saw things that I'd never seen before. I saw dogs burying their own shit as soon as they'd shat and what's more wiping themselves afterwards. I saw waiters tipping bankers and—

DANA

Shall I go on with this?

DUKE

As you wish. (*He continues to pace and hit his hand.*)

DANA

(*Reading*) "I mention these few questions to give you a more definite idea of the content of the study. No previous studies have been done concerning the singer and how his personal relationships are affected by the response to his work. The usual question that the historian or academician asks is how a singer's life affects the content of his work. Here I am concerned with how the reception of his work affects the singer's social environment. I realize how busy you must be but I hope you will consent to being interviewed. The interview should take about one hour. I can assure you of complete anonymity.

I do hope you will participate and I'm looking forward to your reply. Sincerely yours, Daniel Damon."

DUKE

Good, good. Give it here. Let me see. (*He crosses to her and takes the letter, he pulls out a pen and writes on the back of the letter.*)
"Dear Daniel Damon . . ."

DANA

Oh Duke. Don't be silly. Honestly.

DUKE

"In reply to your letter I would like to say thank you very much. Sincerely, Duke Durgens." (*He begins folding the letter into a paper airplane.*)

DANA

You should just turn it in to your manager, that's all. You don't have to reply personally like that. Turn it in to Floyd.

DUKE

Floyd's got work to do.

DANA

Well so do you.

DUKE

So do I. I have work and Floyd has work and there's no gaps in between for anything like replies to Danny Damon. But it must be done. We can't leave old Dan hanging. Not a sociologist, at any rate. Sociologists are movers. They don't hang around waiting for replies. They make up their own if they don't get them on time. And I'd hate to see him do that. To create a lie out of my negligence. (*He rushes downstage and throws the letter out into the audience.* DANA *jumps to her feet.*)

Here it comes, Danny! Watch it come! Don't let it get away! Yoo hoo!

DANA
Duke! What have you done! You ridiculous idiot! You've thrown the letter into the audience. Do you know what that means? That means anyone can pick that letter up and read it! And that means that anyone can pretend to be Duke Durgens and walk right up to Danny Damon and say hello I'm Duke and Danny will say well I'm glad to meet you at last Mr. Durgens and then he'll sit down with Mr. Damon and then they'll just proceed with the interview as though he were you and he'll tell Danny Damon whatever he wants and Mr. Damon will believe him and write it all down and pay him a great deal of money thinking it's you and he'll just leave and go spend it somewhere and there's no way to trace him because they don't know his real name or anything and meanwhile all this fake personal life that he's conjured up and slandered you with will be written down and printed by Daniel Damon and held forever in the private vaults of Corning University forever and ever with no way of our ever getting to read it. You stupid, stupid boy. (FLOYD, DUKE'S *manager, enters wearing shades and a suit; he crosses to the piano, sits, and starts to play "Chopsticks."* DANA *crosses over to him but* FLOYD *keeps playing,* DUKE *just stares at the audience.*)

DANA
Floyd, I'm glad you arrived but Duke is really getting entirely out of hand here recently. He made an airplane out of a letter and threw it away. Can you imagine that?

FLOYD
(*Still playing*) How did you manage that, Dukie?

DUKE
I made the wings and weighted it just right and gave it a little snap with my wrist and away she flew.

DANA

Bad news, Floyd, if that letter ever gets into the hands of a stranger. Anybody could pick that letter up. Anybody at any time. They might even go all the way. With a letter like that you've got a free ticket into almost anything you'd like. Who knows, someone could even start cutting records in Duke's name and get away with it even. Or charge free meals at Duke's expense or—
(*Floyd stops playing and stands slowly, then crosses over to* DUKE *and puts his arm around his shoulders.*)

FLOYD

There's something bigger going on than that, Dana. We can handle that without too much sweat or pain. Right now the thing that bothers us more and more, my colleagues and I, is when will Duke produce for us his next hit tune. When is it that Duke will come to us with a shiny new tune that we can sell. Duke knows of course about his date in Phoenix coming up within the week. And he also knows that that date can be easily filled with his one original, million-dollar, gold-label, award-winning song, "Prisoners, Get up out of Your Homemade Beds," and the rest of the evening can be spent with Duke singing songs from other artists' repertoires, but when is it that Dukie will come to us and say look Floyd I've done it, I've come through, here's my next hit?

DUKE

I don't know, Floyd. I'm stuck.

FLOYD

But he will. It just takes time. And before you know it there it is staring you in the face. It was there all along but he just couldn't see but now he sees with his own two eyes and his eyes light up like never before because he knows he's got it now. He knows he can show it to Floyd and then Floyd can show it to the world and the world will see it for the very first time and the world will say we were just stuck before but now Dukie's come through and shown us the way.

DANA

He's been trying, Floyd. (FLOYD *digs his fingers into the back of* DUKE'S *neck.*)

FLOYD

Then everything just falls off Dukie's back. There's a general relief for Dukie and the pressure he felt in the back of his neck is gone forever and ever. And he doesn't know how to thank himself for that. (*He breaks away from* DUKE *and heads toward the door.*) There'll be two guitarists here at two o'clock sharp and I've told them to be at your complete disposal. They'll give you all the time you need but you'd better use it because they cost twenty-five an hour plus tip so I don't want any clowning around. Dana, you get Duke whatever he needs, coffee or anything, and see that he stays up here until something gets done. And don't bother him about trivia because that's for me and my men to deal with and no one else. Is that clear? I'll be back here at six to see how things are shaping up. Good luck. (*He exits. As soon as he closes the door the band stands and begins this song and* DANA *and* DUKE *do the frug on stage, this song should be loud and fast.*)

#1 BAND SONG
Well ya' grew up small
Then ya' grew up big
And the folks in town
Ask ya' what ya' dig
And ya' said to them
Well I hadn't thought
And they said to you
Don't let yourself get caught
Just jerkin' off behind some dark tree

'Cause the neighbor's kid got caught doin' that
And a' course ya' know where he wound up at
He's now in either

Sing Sing or Alcatraz or either
Sing Sing or Alcatraz or
The county zoo
It's no good for you, boy
It's no good for you.

Then ya' said that sounds pretty scary to me
That's not really the place where I'd like to be
So ya' walked alone for four days straight
Ya' walked alone and ya' grew to hate
All the people in your home town
All the people who brought you down
And ya' walked alone for eight days straight
Till ya' couldn't remember when it was ya' last ate
And ya' still didn't know how to seal your fate
Against the sounds of

Sing Sing or Alcatraz or either
Sing Sing or Alcatraz or
The county zoo
It's no good for you, boy
It's no good for you.

So ya' buried your face in some dark tree
And ya' sighed and gasped what's to become of me
But a man sat smokin' behind his desk
Right above the tree where you lay down to rest
And his voice echoed out right through the trunk
Boy, take my advice and don't believe in that junk
And ya' said okay but what can I do
And he said there's a' lot a' songs that I got for you
And ya' said boy oh boy I can hardly wait
And he said I already got you a date at either

Sing Sing or Alcatraz or either
Sing Sing or Alcatraz or
The county zoo
Just take your pick, boy
It'll be good for you.

Then ya' jumped right up off a' the ground
And you yelled wow when can I start
And he said well first we gotta look around
For somebody who can accompany you
And ya' said I already know just who could do that
It's the neighbor's kid and ya' know where he's at
And he asked where and ya' told him true
Just like the folks in town had once told you
You said he's in either

Sing Sing or Alcatraz or either
Sing Sing or Alcatraz or
The county zoo
Either one I'm sure
Will be fine with you
Either one I'm sure
Will be fine with you.

(DANA *and* DUKE *finish dancing and applaud the band, the band bows and the play continues.*)

DUKE
Dana.

DANA
What?

DUKE
Do you have some scissors around?

DANA
No. Why? (DUKE *reaches into his pocket and pulls out a roll of bills.*)

DUKE

Take this and go downstairs somewhere to a scissors shop and buy a pair and then come right back up.

DANA

What for? (*She takes the money.*)

DUKE

Do as I say! You're supposed to get me what I want.

DANA

All right but you'd better get down to work or it'll be bad news all the way around.

DUKE

Take off, chick!

DANA

Scissors. (*She exits,* DUKE *crosses down and bows to the audience, then sings.*)

DUKE

My baby's gone
Where did she go
I loved her so
Why did she go
She left me by myself
She left me in a trance
And I couldn't even dance for
Days and days.

My baby left
She left me all alone
She didn't leave a bone
For me to chew
I'm so very blue . . .

(*He stomps his foot, the band boos him,* DUKE *gives them the finger,* DANA *enters with scissors.*)

DANA
Scissors.

DUKE
Beautiful. Now cut my hair.

DANA
What! (DUKE *crosses to the sofa and sits.*)

DUKE
I want you to cut off all my hair and then I have a surprise for you.

DANA
Duke, you can't do that. You have a date to do. You can't! You can't! You can't do that.

DUKE
Dana, I'm stuck. You know I'm stuck and I know it. But I have a surprise for everyone. I have a love song to sing but it has to correspond with the way I look or it just won't work. Now please cut my hair or I'll be stuck forever.

DANA
But Duke— (*There is a loud knock at the door.*) Who is it? (*Another knock*)

DUKE
Go see. (DANA *crosses to the door.*)

DANA
Who is it, please? (*A voice comes from the other side.*)

DRAKE'S VOICE
It's Drake, baby. Open up.

DANA
Duke, it's your brother. What shall I do? Oh what shall I do, Duke? Oh what can I do?

DUKE

Let him in. (DANA *opens the door and* DRAKE DURGENS *enters with his friend* CISCO; *they both have long hair, shades, and are dressed exactly like* DUKE.)

DANA

Hello, Drake. (CISCO *goes to the piano and starts playing "Chopsticks."*)

DRAKE

Howdy. Nothing going on here, eh? That's funny, Dukie. Every time we come around here there's nothing going on. How do you account for that?

DUKE

Must be the time of year.

DRAKE

Couldn't be that, baby, since we been here at all seasons and hours and the same nothing keeps going on. Don't you write or something? Don't you sing a little now and then to fill in the gaps?

DANA

Duke works all the time. There aren't any gaps to fill.

DRAKE

Can't expect one song to last you forever, Duke. What's the average duration of a hit like yours? What would you say offhand? Just candidly?

DUKE

I couldn't say. I'm not a sociologist.

DRAKE

I'd make a rough guess of about eight months, maybe nine. No more than that.

DUKE

Could be.

DRAKE
'Course with a swinging head like yours you should have no trouble. You should have the mothers rolling out as fast as they come in. You know, a song a day at the very least. Maybe two if the climate's right. You know, if you're really tuned in to what's going on out in the streets. And given of course if the streets are tuned in to what's going on in the juke box. It's like a circle, Dukie. You got to keep turning. Right?

DANA
Listen, Drake, Duke has to have his hair cut now so if you could go away for a while— (CISCO *stops playing the piano and stands,* DUKE *stands.*)

DUKE
Dana, shut up!

DRAKE
Dukie's cutting his hair? No.

CISCO
You're cutting your hair?

DUKE
Look, Drake, I have some new songs that Floyd needs. I mean I've written a new love song and I need to change my hair for it. You know what I mean?

DRAKE
Sure, baby. I understand.

DUKE
It's not so drastic as all that. It'll grow back again. I'm sure of it.

DRAKE
Sure. Here, Dana, let's have those. (*He takes the scissors from* DANA *and crosses up to* DUKE.) It's not so bad,

Dukie. It'll just be like it was before you decided to let it grow. It'll just be shorter, that's all. (*He backs* DUKE *up until* DUKE *sits back down on the sofa with* DRAKE *standing over him holding the scissors.*) So just relax. Try to think of something else if this bothers you at all. It won't be painful, in any case. And like you say, it'll all grow back in case you change your mind.

DUKE
I know, Drake, but I'm—

DRAKE
Shhhh. Cisco might even sing us a song if we just relax. If we take it easy and don't worry about anything at all. Cisco, what do you say? You sing our song, baby. Our own original song. And I'll cut Dukie's hair and Dukie will just relax and maybe Dana will hum or something. How does that sound, Dana?

DANA
I suppose. But be careful. He has a date to do.

CISCO
What song, Drake?

DRAKE
Sing the song we wrote last year in the bar across the street. The song we wrote at the table where Dukie was with us drinking wine and smiling.

DANA
What song was that?

DRAKE
You weren't there, Dana, but Dukie remembers. Go ahead, Cisco. (CISCO *crosses downstage and picks up the guitar, bows to the audience, and starts to play and sing while* DRAKE *cuts* DUKE'S *hair very short.*)

CISCO
Well early one day you got out a' bed
And then you decided to go to sleep instead
So early one day you got back in the sack
And fell fast asleep in your homemade rack.

Well you don't know how you decided this,
All that you know is there's somethin' you missed
But you don't know what and you don't know where
So you just stay put and ya' go nowhere.

Oh prisoners, won't you get up out a' your homemade
    beds,
Oh prisoners, won't you get up out a' your homemade
    beds.

Well early one night you got so very up tight
And you said this sleepin' it just ain't right
But there was nothin' at all that you could do
'Cause your eyes stayed shut with your homemade glue.

(DANA *starts yelling but* DUKE *just sits and lets* DRAKE
cut his hair as CISCO *continues the song.*)

DANA
Stop it! Stop it! That's Duke's song! Stop singing! Stop
it! I'll call the police!

CISCO
But you couldn't hear your own voice speak
And ya' couldn't walk 'cause your legs was too weak
So ya' lay in bed cryin' to yourself
And your life just sat there hanging on the shelf.

Oh prisoners, get up out a' your homemade beds,
Oh prisoners, get up out a' your homemade beds.

And now the day and night are just the same
And now the light and dark don't have no name

And you just lay in bed without no game
And you just lay there sleepin' without no fame.

But when you do awaken from your deep sleep
The bed will disappear and you won't even weep,
You'll walk right outside without no name,
You'll walk right outside from where you came.

So prisoners, get up out a' your homemade beds,
Oh prisoners, get up out a' your homemade heads.

(*The band applauds,* CISCO *bows.*)

DANA
You lousy bastards! Duke, they stole your song! Duke
wrote that song, not you!

DRAKE
(*Still cutting* DUKE'S *hair while* DUKE *just sits passively.*)
Duke *sold* the song. Didn't you, Dukie?

DANA
He wrote it, too! I remember the night he came home
with it in his head. He came right through that door and
he said darling I have a song! I have a beautiful, beautiful song with a protest message and poetry and everything. And I said I'm so happy and we both sat down
right here and went to work on it. It took us four and
a half hours because I timed it. And when it was done
we played it on the piano and sang it and ran around here
laughing and singing. And we called up this guy named
Floyd and sang it to him over the phone and Floyd said
we'll cut it tomorrow morning early and we did and
within a week it was number ten on the hit parade, then
nine, then eight, then it jumped to number two and at
last by the end of the month it was number one and the
biggest smash hit this country had ever heard or seen
before. Isn't that right, Duke! Ask Duke, he'll tell you.

143

Go ahead and ask him! Ask him. Ask him. Go ahead and ask him.

CISCO
Shall I play another song?

DRAKE
What did you have in mind, Cisco?

CISCO
Something simple.

DANA
No more songs! You both have to go now. Go on! Get out of here! We're expecting a couple musicians to come and help Duke. Now go on! (CISCO *sets down the guitar and goes to the piano and starts playing "Chopsticks" again.*)

DUKE
It's all right, Dana.

DANA
What do you mean! They've accused you, Duke. They've accused you of stealing. Your own brother! Your own brother and your brother's friend. (DUKE *stands with his hair all cut and crosses to her while* CISCO *continues to play "Chopsticks."*)

DUKE
Dana, I want you to do me a favor. I want you to throw everything you heard out of your head and go downstairs and buy me a black suit and tie and some black shoes and a white shirt. I want you to do that now and come back as fast as you can. Please. It's very important. (*He pulls out another roll of bills and hands it to her.*)

DANA
You really did steal that song, didn't you! (*She takes the money.*)

144

DUKE

Now go on, Dana.

DANA

You did! You stole it from your very own brother. I remember now because when you came in that night you said your brother was singing this groovy song but you had a better one. It was the same one, though! It was! How could you, Duke!

DUKE

No, Dana. That night I was taking a walk with Floyd. Now go get my suit!

DANA

I'm not your flunky! Go buy your own suit! (*She throws the money at* DUKE *and turns to go out the door as* FLOYD *enters.*)

FLOYD

Great! Do I have to get a special guardian to guard you people and watch you to make sure you do your work? Is that what I have to do? All right! I'll do it. (*He opens the door and whistles,* CISCO *continues to play "Chopsticks."*) Peter! On the double! (PETER, *a bodyguard, enters wearing a guard's uniform complete with pistol and badge and holding a billy club; he also wears shades.*)

DANA

Floyd, Duke's an impostor. He stole that song that's made you rich. It isn't even his.

FLOYD

This is Peter. He's completely trained and attuned to— stop that silly music! (CISCO *stops.*) I hired you clowns to accompany Duke, not to piddle around on the piano.

DUKE

You hired my brother! You hired my brother to accompany me! (*He lunges at* FLOYD *but* PETER *steps in and hits him on the head with the club,* DUKE *falls to the ground,* DANA *screams.*)

DANA

Duke! You've killed him! You've killed him! You've killed my Duke. (*She kneels at his side, sobbing.*)

FLOYD

Shut up, broad. He'll come to in a second and then you can all get down to business. I said I wanted a new song and I'm going to get one.

DANA

Not out of Duke! He'll never sing again!

FLOYD

Then somebody else. How about you? (*He crosses to* DRAKE.)

DRAKE

I accompany, I don't sing. (DANA *rises.*)

DANA

Don't believe him, Floyd. He sings. In fact he sings very well. He even writes his own tunes. Original ones.

FLOYD

Original, eh? Well let's hear some. What's your name, boy?

DRAKE

Cisco.

FLOYD

Well, Cisco, who knows, we may even have a date for you in Phoenix if you have what it takes.

DANA

He's Duke's brother, Floyd. His name is Drake Durgens.

DRAKE
Actually Drake writes all the songs and I just accompany. (FLOYD *turns to* CISCO.)

FLOYD
Is that right? Well Drake, could you sing a few for us?

CISCO
I just did.

DANA
It's the other way around. He's Cisco, not Drake. They're lying to you, Floyd!

FLOYD
What difference? He has a song that he'd like to sing and we'd like to hear it. Right, Drake?

CISCO
I just sang it.

FLOYD
Well, sing it again, boy.

DANA
No! If you sing that song, Cisco, I'll kill you! That's not your song! You have no right to sing that song.

FLOYD
Peter! Take this girl and hold her and then take out your pistol and put it to her head and if these guys don't sing by the time I count to five, then pull the trigger. (PETER *follows his instructions.*)

DANA
No! You can't sing that song! That's not your song! They stole Duke's song, Floyd! (PETER *covers her mouth and holds the pistol to her head.*)

FLOYD
One! Two! Three! Four! Five! (PETER *fires the pistol, it*

147

makes a tremendous boom, DANA *falls to the floor.*) What did you do! What in the hell did you do!

PETER
I pulled the trigger.

FLOYD
You pulled the trigger! Do you realize what you've done! Look at what you've done!

PETER
I know.

FLOYD
Are you two going to play ball now or not? Look what's happened on account of your negligence. (DUKE *starts to groan and slowly gets up, rubbing his head;* FLOYD *rushes to him and helps him up.*) Dukie! Oh Dukie baby, they've killed your girl. They've killed your sweet little girl by just plain old not cooperating. Look what they've done to Dana, Dukie. Just look at that. Isn't that a shame?

DUKE
She's dead. Oh my God.

FLOYD
Yes, Duke, I'm afraid so.

DUKE
Did she get my suit?

FLOYD
Your suit? (CISCO *crosses to the piano again and starts to play "Chopsticks";* DRAKE *crosses up to* DANA *and kneels down beside her as* DUKE *walks around the stage in a daze, followed by* FLOYD.)

DUKE
She was going to get a suit. Black with a tie and white shirt with black shining shoes and buttons.

FLOYD

Duke! What has happened to your hair! Oh my God! (DUKE *feels his hair*.)

DUKE

It's there. It's always there. In the summer it's short and grows long in the winter on account of the changing climate. I never have to do a thing. It just corresponds itself to the climate and that's that. I never knew anything like it before. But it's been going on for as long as I can remember.

FLOYD

Phoenix, Duke! What will they say in Phoenix? They won't even know who you are. They'll laugh you right off the stage!

DUKE

I tell them look, I've been around for a century with changing hair on my head. My pubic hair remains constant but the head manages by itself. It comes and goes. Long and short. Thick and thin. And there's nothing to do about that. If you lose your hair it's gone and you just realize one day that it's thinner than before. That's all.

FLOYD

Stop playing that music! (CISCO *stops, the band stands and begins this song which should be slower and somewhat softer than the first, all the actors dance individually around the stage except* DANA *who remains dead on the floor*.)

#2 BAND SONG

Well now that you're older than ya' was before
And ya' can tell that you're older
'Cause everything is a bore
Well now that you're clumsy instead of so quick

And now that your head
Seems to make your stomach sick

Who'll open the door
While you lay on the floor,
Who'll brush your long hair
While you just sit and stare
At the friends all around you
Who pump you and pound you
For the truth you can't see
For either them or either me
'Cause we're sunk on the ground
And your heart don't even pound
While you lay on the floor
And they just ask you for more
Of the same that ya' gave,
Of the same that they took,
But they all want a look
At the black secret book
That ya' lost from your hand
When your hand hit the page
And the page turned to fire
And the fire burned your arm
And your arm burned your chest
And all of your lovin' friends they all know the rest

So now that you're down flat on the ground
All of your friends create the sound,
All of your pals create the pound
Of the sound of the song that they all want you to hear
But your ears can't begin
'Cause they're all jammed up with tears
From your eyes that both watch the years
And the years that watch your eyes disguise your fears
So please tell me now when they ask you for more
Who'll open the door

While you lay on your back,
Who'll destroy your pride
While ya' lay on your side,
Who'll ease you with grace
While ya' lay on your face,
Who'll coax your short hair
So it doesn't stay bare,
Who'll give you the sign to resign from your sleep,
Who'll give you some sleep to resign from the test
Of your arm and your chest
That got burned with the rest
When your zest turned to jelly
Inside of your belly
But don't worry now, whatever you do,
Just do your dance and forget about who

So now that you're younger
Than ya' was before
And ya' can tell that you're younger
'Cause ya' don't mind the floor
Where you crawl up and down
With your nose to the ground
And ya' don't mind the smell
'Cause you can't even tell
The difference 'tween heaven and hell any more
And the floor and the sky
Shine right through your eye
And ya' sigh and ya' groan
But ya' can't pick the bone
Of the dead that won't die
And their sigh and their groan
Match right with the tone of your own
But don't worry now, whatever you do,
Just do your dance and forget about who,
Just say your prayers and go softly upstairs,
Just eat your food 'cause nobody cares,

And nobody dares to say prayers in the street
And the street doesn't care if ya' just sit and eat
So eat while ya' can and it all might come true
'Cause who is around who can tell what to do
And who is around who can save you from you,
Who is around who can save you from you?

(*They finish dancing and applaud the band, then continue the play.*)

FLOYD
All right! You asked for it and now you're going to get it. You two guys were hired by me. Right? I paid you money in advance to accompany my boy here. But now my boy has lost his hair and he's in no shape to cope with Phoenix. So seeing as how you both are paid in advance for a job you haven't done, you're both going to Phoenix in place of my boy. From now on your name is Duke Durgens. You got that?

CISCO
Roger. (*He salutes.*)

FLOYD
And your name is whatever it already is.

DRAKE
Cisco.

FLOYD
Right. So you'd both better just accept that right now. Now Peter will get you whatever you want but I'm leaving specific instructions with Peter not to let either of you out of this room without my okay.

DRAKE
What about her?

FLOYD
I'll have some men sent by to take the body away some-

where. Peter, don't let either of them out and don't let anyone in unless it's me or my men. Do you understand? Do I make myself clear?

PETER

Roger. (*He salutes.*)

FLOYD

And don't use that gun again or it'll be the end of your job. In fact, give it to me now and I'll keep it for you in a safe place.

PETER

I don't know. We're not supposed to let unauthorized personnel touch or handle any of our—

FLOYD

Give me the gun, Peter! (PETER *takes the pistol out and hands it to* FLOYD.) That's a boy. And you two had better come up with some new songs or it'll be bad news for you both. Good luck. (*He exits,* PETER *starts hitting the club against the palm of his hand.*)

PETER

Stand back away from the body, Cisco. (DRAKE *moves away.*)

DRAKE

My name is Drake, if you don't mind. Drake Durgens.

PETER

Let me tell you all something to start things off with. First of all, I'm thoroughly trained and attuned to every possible kind of devious methods and trickery that you could possibly pull as a means of escape and/or assault. (*He begins moving around the stage, slapping the club into his palm more firmly.*) I have no doubts that you know more than me either collectively or individually. It may even be possible that singly or collectively you may be even smarter than me in certain areas or even in most areas but not in the most important one for this precise time and place and situation. In this particularly unique circumstance I have everything in my control simply because I was once in a position exactly like yourselves. Given that one simple little historical fact, I now have indisputably the upper hand. Not simply because I have a weapon but because I exhausted every possible avenue of escape once myself when I was exactly like you are now. And I tried every one. I tried possibility after possibility over a period of ten years until at last one of them worked. The very last one. And I was free for the very first time. So you see, here I am. The one and only person here who knows what that possibility is and the one and only person who won't tell. And the one and only person to stop any one of you if you happen to accidentally come across it, either singly or collectively. And God help you if you do.

DUKE

Look, Peter, my name's Duke and I'm a singer and—

PETER

I know your names. There's no need for introductions here.

DUKE

I'm not introducing. I'm telling you my actual life. I was a singer, a very popular singer with very long hair, a girl friend, and a song that I stole from my brother Drake over a bottle of wine across the street. But nobody knew that and the song became a fantastic hit, a beautiful smashing hit. I was admired from coast to coast by the people dearest to me and closest to my heart. By the people of my generation. I was admired and cherished because the song was true and good and reflected accurately the emotions, thoughts, and feelings of our time

154

and place. (*The band cheers.*) Thank you. But it was
the only song I had. The only one. And I became stuck,
Peter. I got stuck somewhere in the middle between—
(*He crosses up to the photographs and points first to
Bob Dylan and then to Robert Goulet.*) Between him
and him. Somewhere almost right in the middle and
everyone was crying for a brand-new song. For a song
like the one I'd sung before or even just for any song.
So I made up a love song and cut my hair so I'd look like
a lover. (*The band boos.*) And then the theft of my un-
original song was revealed and my girl was killed and
my brother was hired to accompany me and Floyd said
I couldn't go to Phoenix looking like this, without any
hair and without a song. So you see, I have no business
here any more. I'm only in your way so I'd like permis-
sion to leave, please. I'm not stuck any more, Peter, and
I'd just like to leave before Floyd gets back. (*He breaks
down in tears.*)

PETER
I suppose you figure the simplicity of your plea would
give the impression to anyone of absolute sincerity but
I can see right through that to the real truth of the matter and it turns out to be a lie.

DUKE
Peter, there's no reason to keep me here! I have no business here!

DRAKE
He's right, Peter. He's my brother and I can vouch for
that. He's telling you the truth.

CISCO
Me too. Even though he's a thief, he's telling the truth.

PETER
Oh well, all right. Step right up, Dukie old boy. Just step

155

right out the door there. You're free to go now. I mean, you have all these vouchers and everything so help yourself.

DUKE
Really?

PETER
Of course. Be my guest. Right this way.

DUKE
Thanks a lot. Thanks, Drake. Cisco. I hope things turn out all right in Phoenix. Say good-bye to Floyd for me, will you? And I'm sorry about the song and everything.

DRAKE
Sure thing, Duke. Good luck.

CISCO
So long. (DUKE *makes for the door and* PETER *slugs him on the back of the head with the club,* DUKE *falls to the ground.*)

DRAKE
That was pretty shitty, Peter.

PETER
I've decided you two should sit together on the couch and also that you should put your hands on top of your heads as an added precaution. (*They do so and cross to the sofa and sit.*)

CISCO
We're supposed to be working, Peter. We have a date in Phoenix coming up soon. We can't just clown around.

PETER
Don't worry about that. As soon as we're clear on where we stand, then we'll start thinking about work.

DRAKE
Floyd's coming back pretty soon and it'll be bad news all the way around if we don't have something new for him to hear.

PETER
We'll have something. Just sit tight. But first of all I have a personal question I'd like to ask you boys before we do anything else.

DRAKE
What do you mean? (PETER *walks up and down in front of them, slapping the club into his palm.*)

PETER
I'd like to redirect the attention for just a moment and turn it off of you and onto me. Just for a change. I'd like to ask you both what you think of me as a person. Just frankly. Don't be afraid of hurting my feelings or anything like that. Just tell me what you think.

CISCO
Well—

PETER
I'd like Cisco to answer first, please.

CISCO
I'm Cisco.

PETER
Now don't start that shit, goddam it! I'm giving you both a chance to relax and feel more comfortable in this already slightly uncomfortable situation and what do you do! You start pulling shit with me! All right. Now then. Give yourself a moment to catch your breath, Cisco, and answer my question as best as you can.

DRAKE
Well I think—

PETER
Just relax for a second and then start in. Don't start in
right off the bat. Now are you ready?

DRAKE
Yes.

PETER
Then answer me!

DRAKE
I think you're a fairly nice guy, Peter, but—

PETER
Now don't give me bullshit generalities. "Nice guy," that
fits anyone. Anyone's a nice guy.

DRAKE
I know but you're a specific kind.

PETER
What kind?

DRAKE
Well—

CISCO
Peter, maybe if you told us a little about your past life,
then maybe we could be more accurate. You could fill in
the gaps, so to speak.

PETER
Didn't I just say I wanted Cisco's answer and not yours.

CISCO
I guess.

PETER
But you answered, didn't you! Didn't you! Answer me!

CISCO
Yes.

PETER
You can go now. I want to be alone with Cisco. I said you could go!

CISCO
All right. You're not going to hit me?

PETER
Drake, don't be silly.

CISCO
All right. (CISCO *gets up and crosses to the door,* PETER *watches him;* CISCO *turns the doorknob but the door won't open, he tries again.*)

CISCO
The door's locked, Peter.

PETER
Don't be silly. (*Peter crosses to the door and opens it wide.*) There, you see.

CISCO
Oh. Thanks. So long.

PETER
Have a good time, Drake. (CISCO *makes to go out the door and* PETER *slugs him with his club,* CISCO *falls to the ground,* DRAKE *stands.*) Sit back down, there! (DRAKE *sits again with his hands on his head;* PETER *pulls* CISCO *into the room and shuts the door, then crosses slowly back up to* DRAKE.)

DRAKE
Look, I really have to get down to work before Floyd gets back.

PETER
We will, Cisco. We'll work all we want just as soon as you answer my question. It's a very simple question really.

All it requires is an unbiased opinion of my character. There's no right or wrong answer in this case. It's just a straightforward opinion. That's all. Then you're free to work.

DRAKE
Well I've known you such a short time, Peter. It seems so—

PETER
I know, Cisco. You're right. In that case I feel somewhat obligated to fill you in on my brief background. Now listen very carefully and see what you can pick up. Anything at all that might be helpful in your answering. One night, several years ago when I was sixteen, I'd just arrived in a very huge city. It doesn't matter which one. (*He begins pacing slowly around the stage, slapping his club.*) The point is I'd come out of the hills where I'd lived up until that point with my father and two brothers and several sheep. On this particular night I was walking along very early in the morning by myself with nobody else around. I'd been walking for quite some time, listening to my steps, when I suddenly saw this man about a block ahead of me crawling along the curb and coughing very loud. I didn't change my pace at all but nevertheless gradually caught up to him since he was crawling very slowly and not making much headway at all. When I got alongside of him I just kept my eyes straight ahead and kept at my constant pace but I could hear him coughing and crawling along the curb. Well I'd walked maybe twenty yards when I discovered he was still alongside me but I hadn't looked down this whole time. I could just hear him crawling along and hacking away and it even made me feel slightly good. Like having a dog at your side in the early morning. Do you see what I mean?

DRAKE

Yes.

PETER

Well that comforting feeling lasted for a while but then began to leave me and be substituted by a kind of panic since by this time I'd walked some sixty yards and the man was still with me. I decided to speed up my pace a bit and even got to the point where I was jogging but all the time he was right at my side and his coughing changed to panting and his crawling changed to trotting. So I stopped, thinking he'd go right on by and disappear up the street, but he stopped too and there was a long time while the both of us just stayed in one place, not seeing each other but knowing we were both there. Then I turned my head just slightly over my shoulder and sort of glanced down into his face and his face had no eyes. Mind you, they weren't eyes that had gone bad and closed up or white eyes that were glazed over or eyes like a blind man has. There weren't any eyes there at all. Just a mouth and nose and ears and everything else. Then I asked him what he wanted with me and why he was tagging along and if I could be of any help at all. And he spoke very clearly without any accent at all and no trace of slurred vowels or consonants. He was perfectly sober and he asked me if I'd please bend down and read the address to him off a metal tag he had hanging from his neck on a silver chain. And I said why not and bent down and held the tag in the palm of my hand and read the only word that was on the tag. I read "Arizona" to him very loudly in his left ear for fear he was deaf, but he wasn't since he jumped a little at the sound. Then he asked if I would please point him in the right direction for Arizona and I said of course and turned him around the opposite way and patted him on the back and off he went on all fours. I watched him for quite some time going right up the middle of the street and getting smaller and smaller when suddenly I felt this hand on my right shoulder and jumped slightly and turned and looked right at the face of this very old policeman in a long blue coat and a badge and a hat and boots and a club and a gun and he said to me was that a friend of yours and I said no and then he asked what business I had with him. So I told him what I just told you. Word for word. Exactly, precisely, without leaving one thing out. Without even coloring it to be in my favor. And then he put his hand around the back of my neck and dug his thumb into one side and the rest of his fingers into the other side and he led me by the neck into the doorway of a building where everyone was fast asleep. He led me right down this hallway by the back of my neck and there were only a couple of lights and he took me way in the back behind this staircase where everything was damp and dark and told me to take off my pants. (*There is a loud knock at the door,* PETER *jumps,* DRAKE *stands up.*) Sit back down there! (DRAKE *sits.*) Who is it!

VOICE
We come to get the body! Floyd sent us.

PETER
There ain't no body here! You got the wrong door!

VOICE
It's the right number! This is where we're supposed to come, all right!

PETER
You better get away from here or we'll call a cop!

VOICE
Look, buster. Floyd told us you was a knucklehead and we might have to break the door down! So open up or we'll do what he says!

PETER
I have specific instructions not to let anyone in or out! I
don't know you! You could be anyone. How do I know
who you are?

VOICE
Well we'll go get Floyd then and you'll see who we are.

PETER
Go ahead!

VOICE
You'll be sorry, punk!

DRAKE
Peter, we have to do something before he gets back. He's
a desperate man. He needs a new song and he'll stop at
nothing to get it.

PETER
You're probably right. But you haven't answered my
question yet and until you do there'll be no chance at all
to learn anything new. (*Peter unbuttons his pants and
takes them off while* DRAKE *stays seated on the sofa.*)

DRAKE
What can I say? I like you very much.

PETER
That explains nothing to me. I want to know what I'm
like, that's all. Not anything else.

DRAKE
Well that's part of it, though. If you like someone it's
usually because they're nice. I mean, I don't like any
bad guys.

PETER
You don't?

DRAKE
Well no. Do you?

PETER
I never met one. (*As soon as he's taken off his pants he crosses to the piano and starts to play "Chopsticks" while* DRAKE *stays sitting on the sofa.*)

DRAKE
It seems like you could get someone else to tell you what you're like. Someone who knows you better. Someone who's close to you and lived with you for a while. I mean what do you want, Peter? I've never done this kind of thing before. Peter! (DRAKE *stands but* PETER *keeps playing "Chopsticks."*) We're in a dangerous situation here! The two of us. They're not going to treat you any different than they are me. When Floyd gets back he's going to be pretty pissed off at you for locking his men out. He's going to knock you down the same as me. In fact he'll probably hire you on to go with me to Phoenix, seeing as how you play the piano so well and also now that Cisco's out of commission. Peter, are you listening to me! (*Drake starts moving slowly toward* PETER *as* PETER *continues to play, ignoring* DRAKE). This is no joke! I can't give you what you want because I don't know what it is. I can't just make it up. I could, I guess. Do you want me to make it up, Peter? Peter! (PETER *stops playing abruptly, there is a loud knock on the door;* PETER *wheels around on the piano stool and grabs* DRAKE, *he puts his hand over* DRAKE'S *mouth and bends one of* DRAKE'S *arms behind his back.*)

FLOYD'S VOICE
Peter! This is Floyd and his men! Now listen, we know you're inside there! And I realize that I gave you specific instructions to let no one in and no one out but now I'm

telling you the opposite. I'm telling you to let us in. Do you hear me, Peter! Open this door.

PETER
The problem is I can't be sure if you're Floyd or if you're more likely just some imposter who's trying to mosey in on a good deal.

FLOYD
What good deal! There's nothing in there that could possibly be of any value to anyone but me. Now let me in this door! (*The door shakes violently.*)

PETER
I'm sorry. I'm thoroughly trained and attuned to every possible—

FLOYD
All right, meat-head! You're through! Finished! Washed up! Down the river! I'm going out to get some cops and when I get back your thorough training ain't going to be worth a hill of beans! You'll be blackballed from every guard corporation in the country! You'll never work again and that's a promise! Come on. (*Peter slowly lets go of* DRAKE, *they face each other.*)

DRAKE
I told you. (PETER *hits him in the stomach with his club,* DRAKE *doubles over.*)

PETER
You'd better think of something fast, boy. There's no telling what they'll do when they get back. Once they break down that door and come in here with guns.

DRAKE
Just let me sing a song, Peter.

PETER
You haven't answered my question yet.

DRAKE

I can't! Don't you see, I can't! I like you very much! I've
told you that. I've told you you're a nice guy!

PETER

Good! (*He slugs* DRAKE *in the back with the club.*) Now
what am I like when you look in my face!

DRAKE

I can't see you, Peter!

PETER

Come on, boy. They'll be back very soon. You can't beat
around the bush at a time like this. In a moment of crisis.

DRAKE

What do you want me to say?

PETER

Say whatever you'd say if you happened to be walking
down the street alone, by yourself, and just accidentally
ran across me in the dark.

DRAKE

But I didn't.

PETER

Pretend you saw me in a flash and we had a short en-
counter and then someone came up and asked you what
you thought of that man you were just now talking to.
What was he like, that man?

DRAKE

Peter, I can't! I'm stuck!

PETER

And then you say whatever just comes into your head in
that split second. Whatever happens to be sitting there in
your memory of the second before and it just spiels out

trippingly off the tongue. It just gushes out in its most accurate way. Word for word, without a moment's hesitation to calculate where it's going or how or why. It just falls out into the air and disappears as soon as it's heard. That's what I want to hear! That's what I want you to say to me. Right now, before it's too late!

PETER

DRAKE

Just let me sing a song, Peter. Please. Let me make up a song for Floyd.

PETER

That'll save your skin but how about mine? What do you suggest for me, meat-head?

DRAKE

You could open the door. You could leave the door wide open so that when they arrive they won't be so mad at you.

PETER

Why not? (*He slugs* DRAKE *again across the back,* DRAKE *falls to all fours.*)

DRAKE

Wait! They—when they see the door wide open they're liable to cool down and then they won't be so rough on you, Peter, because they'll think you thought it over and reconsidered. Maybe they will.

PETER

Maybe you're right, Drake. Maybe that's a good idea. (*He goes to the door and opens it wide,* DRAKE *starts moving slowly around the stage on all fours as* PETER *follows him.*) There! Now you'd better get down to work, boy. You'd better think up a new song, now that my skin's saved. By the way, thanks very much. I never would have thought of that possibility. The open-door routine.

Chicago and Other Plays

DRAKE

That's all right. (DRAKE *paces faster on all fours as* PETER *crosses slowly to the sofa and sits next to the radio.*)

PETER

I'm not much good on songs, though. Wish I was, though, so I could help you out. I could play a little something on the piano if you want. Just something to help you get started.

DRAKE

No, I'm all right. I'll be okay. (*He paces faster up and down the apron of the stage while* PETER *just sits on the sofa, slapping the club in his lap.*)

PETER

It wouldn't be anything fancy, Drake. All I know is the simple stuff. But it might be just enough to kick something off for you. To get the wheels turning, so to speak. I'm sure glad I'm not in your shoes.

DRAKE

No, it's all right. It's coming. (DRAKE *starts humming some kind of tune now.*)

PETER

Must be really something to have that kind of facility. To be able to make up a song whenever you feel like it. Just on the spur of the moment like that. How about the radio, Drake? That might do the trick. What do you say? (PETER *turns on the radio as* DRAKE *continues to pace up and down more frantically;* PETER *just sits on the sofa, slapping the club in his lap, as the following comes from the radio.*)

RADIO: DANIEL DAMON'S VOICE

So I do hope we have given all of you somewhat of an indication of just exactly how the personal life of an

168

artist is affected and/or altered by the reception of his work by the public at large. And we would like to thank our special guest tonight, Mr. Duke Durgens, for being so cooperative in this survey of ours and to wish him all the luck in the world. Duke, it's been a pleasure. DUKE DURGEN'S VOICE Thank you, Danny. DANNY'S VOICE And now we would like to close out this evening's session of the Corning Interview Hour with the sensational sound of the number one hit tune in the world. Thank you for joining us and until next week this is Dan Damon saying— (*The song should break in extremely loud, over the radio.*)

Well early one day you got out a' bed
And then you decided to go to sleep instead
So early one day you got back in the sack
And fell fast asleep in your homemade rack

Well you don't know how you decided this,
All that you know is there's somethin' you missed
But you don't know what and you don't know where
So you just stay put and ya' go nowhere.

(DUKE *gets up slowly and rubs his head, then exits quietly out the door;* PETER *stays sitting on the sofa, keeping time to the song with his club;* DRAKE *continues pacing up and down; the band joins the radio at this point and sings along with it to the end.*)

Oh prisoners, won't you get up out a' your homemade beds
Oh prisoners, won't you get up out a' your homemade beds.

Well early one night you got so very up tight
And you said this sleepin' it just ain't right
But there was nothin' at all that you could do
'Cause your eyes stayed shut with your homemade glue.

169

But you couldn't hear your own voice speak
And ya' couldn't walk 'cause your legs was too weak
So ya' lay in bed cryin' to yourself
And your life just sat there hanging on the shelf.

(CISCO *gets up slowly and rubs his head, then exits quietly out the door; the song continues.*)

Oh prisoners, get up out a' your homemade beds
Oh prisoners, get up out a' your homemade beds.

And now the day and night are just the same
And now the light and dark don't have no name
And you just lay in bed without no game
And you just lay there sleepin' without no fame

But when you do awaken from your deep sleep
The bed will disappear and you won't even weep,
You'll walk right outside without no name,
You'll walk right outside from where you came.

(DANA *gets up slowly and yawns, then exits quietly.*)

So prisoners, get up out a' your homemade beds
Oh prisoners, get up out a' your homemade heads.

(*The song finishes, the band stops,* PETER *turns off the radio as* DRAKE *continues pacing,* PETER *gets up slowly and crosses to the door, he slams the door shut and turns to* DRAKE; DRAKE *freezes in place staring at* PETER, *who crosses to* DRAKE *and stands over him for a while, tapping the club in his palm, then suddenly raises the club to hit* DRAKE; *there is a loud knock at the door, the LIGHTS BLACK OUT.*)

The End